KEEPING CATS

TS-219

Photography: Isabelle Francais, E. Gelduldig, Dorothy Holby, Ingeborg's Animals (Aschermann, Caspersen, Grell, Heitmann, Kurze, Liebold, Putz, T. Rausch, Reinhard, H. Reinhard), W. Layer, Robert Pearcy, Vereins Deutscher Katzenfreunde.

Drawings: Milada Krautmann, Marianne Golte-Bechtle.

Originally published in German by Franckh-Kosmos Verlags-GmbH & Co. under the title *Katzen*. First edition © 1991 by Franckh-Kosmos Verlags-GmbH & Co., Stuttgart.

Distributed in the UNITED STATES to the Pet Trade by T.F.H. Publications, Inc., One T.F.H. Plaza, Neptune City, NJ 07753; distributed in the UNITED STATES to the Bookstore and Library Trade by National Book Network, Inc. 4720 Boston Way, Lanham MD 20706; in CANADA to the Pet Trade by H & L Pet Supplies Inc., 27 Kingston Crescent, Kitchener, Ontario N2B 2T6; Rolf C. Hagen Ltd., 3225 Sartelon Street, Montreal 382 Quebec; in CANADA to the Book Trade by Macmillan of Canada (A Division of Canada Publishing Corporation), 164 Commander Boulevard, Agincourt, Ontario M1S 3C7; in ENGLAND by T.F.H. Publications, PO Box 15, Waterlooville PO7 6BQ; in AUSTRALIA AND THE SOUTH PACIFIC by T.F.H. (Australia), Pty. Ltd., Box 149, Brookvale 2100 N.S.W., Australia; in NEW ZEALAND by Brooklands Aquarium Ltd. 5 McGiven Drive, New Plymouth, RD1 New Zealand; in Japan T.F.H. Publications, Japan—Jiro Tsuda, 10-12-3 Ohjidai, Sakura, Chiba 285, Japan; in SOUTH AFRICA by Multipet Pty. Ltd., P.O. Box 35347, Northway, 4065, South Africa. Published by T.F.H. Publications, Inc.
MANUFACTURED IN THE UNITED STATES OF AMERICA
BY T.F.H. PUBLICATIONS, INC.

KEEPING CATS

Gerd Schmitt-Hausser

A mixed-breed kitty enjoying the great outdoors.

Contents

Introduction

I really wanted to begin to write a book about cats, but my typewriter keyboard is occupied by a large striped toy belonging to Mowgli, my yearling Birman tomcat. Mowgli regards all the activities in this household socially burdensome if they don't involve him personally. That includes the reading of books and newspapers, cooking, eating, morning and evening washing and dressing, housecleaning, moving things around, and even those things we humans of both sexes do from time to time which absolutely do not require the presence of a cat!

Mowgli doesn't really want to participate, only do away with the undesirable activities. It's rather impossible, for example, to turn the page of a newspaper or book when close to nine pounds of attractively packaged plush fur is laying on it. It's difficult too for an experienced cooking hobbyist to finely dice an onion with a large knife when the above-mentioned paw wants to play ball with the onion. Likewise, it's a problem to use a modern vacuum cleaner when a four-legged animal's hunting instinct is triggered by it. In contrast to his two feline house mates, Bagheera and Einstein, this stubborn blockhead is not even afraid of a vacuum cleaner, which all cat's are rightly supposed to be.

Fortunately, even this activist in cat's clothing has a cat's normal need for sleep, that is, fourteen to sixteen hours a day. Unfortunately, he takes his naps at times when there's nothing going on in the house anyway. When anything does happen, he's wide awake and right there in the middle of it.

Talking about being awake, I awoke from a wild nightmare in which my cats were being pursued by gigantic dogs uttering ghastly screeches. Bagheera, our red-blond Abyssinian, and Mowgli were sitting next to our bed, where my wife had buried her head under her pillow. Bagheera cheeped-cheeped in a nervous staccato. Mowgli gave forth with variously modulated siren calls. Their purpose was clear: the cat door that leads outside was closed for the night, and our cats wanted it opened. Well, we had been half awake for at least an hour, which was why I had a nightmare. I half dreamt that a wild chase was tearing through our bedroom and that our gray-speckled tom Einstein was involved. This inveterate individualist meanwhile made himself comfortable up against my legs and made no reference to any door-opening time. A glance at the alarm clock told me it was 6:30 am.

I mumbled 'No, too early,' and rolled over on my other

side. Then, instead of simply waking up, I sat bolt upright in my bed. Einstein had started to play with my feet without first retracting his claws. His two comrades had meanwhile remembered that I'm a worthy object to awaken, and they once again squeaked. It was 7:00 am. Pure extortion. To get even another wink of sleep, I finally had to let them out. With a groan, I rolled out of bed, and all three tails shot straight up to salute me. Mowgli threw his bullish head against my right leg, Einstein rubbed his rear against my left leg, and Bagheera gave me an expressive sigh. 'He finally got the idea!' was written all over their faces. They quickly appeased me, and I headed for the cat door, but they dashed off down the

long hallway to the kitchen, so I had to follow them. Their feeding bowls were empty. I shuffled around in a drawer for the can opener, took down a can of the good stuff, veal stew, and finally got it open, but not before I sliced my index finger on the sharp top of the can. Now I was really awake and managed to fill the three bowls...which by no means meant that each cat ate out of its own bowl. Not at all. Each had to constantly check whether the neighbor's meal was any better. How human! Then it all went remarkably well. If one was shoved rather rudely, he took it good-naturedly...until the next chance to get even.

Breakfast didn't last long, for a few mouthfuls were always there for them overnight as emergency

Cats don't like it when their human companions travel. Many cats clearly realize the meaning of an open suitcase and try to obstruct coming events.

rations, and off they trotted towards the cat door. Bagheera carefully took his bearings then slipped out through the cat doorway, but not without first reviewing a playful paw swipe from Einstein on his rump. They all traipsed through the flap door then sat nicely staggered on the garden steps.

I crawled back into bed and dozed off a few minutes before a flap-flap roused me rudely again. Someone came back in. I listened with my heart in my mouth, waiting for cat wailing that signaled some dire encounter with an enemy, torn ears, infected bites in the head...all of the things we've already gone through. No, none of that. All quiet, then another flap-flap signaled that the returnee had gone out again. That was most probably Einstein, who regularly shuttles in and out while the other two disappear for an hour or two, most likely to catch a few winks of cat nap, but with eye and ear alert to any movement nearby.

So I rolled over on my side and slept soundly for another hour until the cat door went into action again, this time resounding in a wild staccato.

> **Nothing is more relaxing than to watch a cat cleaning itself.**

The neighbor's dog had barked from inside his house but that sufficed to recall all my scared cats from the far-flung corners of their territory and send them safely through the cat door once again. Mowgli sprang up on the window sill to try for a look at the neighboring dog creature. Bagheera was more cautious and crawled right under the bed. Einstein made himself comfortable against my legs and began to play the clawing game with my toes again. Sleep was out of the question.

So, at least I could start work. Now, here I sit but can't use my typewriter because Mowgli has his paws on the keys. I scribble my thoughts down on a pad, fully knowing that I won't be able to decipher it tomorrow. There, Mowgli finally lets me get at my keyboard...but Einstein is brushing up against my legs to ask for a few bites of dry cat food as his reward for going out to do his duties, something that just stayed on as a habit.

Bagheera is trying to clamber up the scratching post to reach the top of the built-in cabinet in the bedroom. The stupid post is poorly constructed and wobbles, sending Bagheera tumbling down. He lands on all fours, naturally, since he's a cat, but he still glowers at me reproachfully. So I get up and hold the scratching post securely until he gracefully pops up to his favorite lookout seat up on top of the cabinet. I've really got to sketch a diagram of the ideal scratching post and have my carpenter friend make one for me. And today I've got to give all three of the cats their second worming dose. I really should start writing now....

You'll say I'm a cat fanatic who is a slave to his cats, and rightfully demand to know when do I finally get to work? Or am I really a professional cat owner or perhaps even a breeder? I'm neither one. Cat fanatic, however, I'll admit to, for I'm crazy about my three beauties. (My wife is even a crazier about them, which is something that I, as the allegedly more rational sex, occasionally criticize her for.)

I consider myself a completely normal cat enthusiast who perhaps has learned a little more than many others about these pussyfooted creatures.

When we first started to share our home with cats twenty-years ago, we certainly didn't realize what we were letting ourselves in for. We were, so to say, as yet untouched by cats. There were many questions and as many problems. We didn't always find answers, despite the ample literature on cats. Since I'm (a) curious and (b) a writer, I decided to gather the whole thing together myself and write a book about it. When I read that book over again today, I'm astonished about what my informants and I didn't know yet about the subject. Nor could we have known in some cases, for only a few scientists dedicate themselves to the systematic study of house cats. Even vets were, as a rule, more knowledgeable about treating dogs than about treating cats. That's changed in the favor of cats since then.

In those days I was much more naive about the care of cats. The more one knows, for example, about cat diseases, the more one worries. Even such concepts as indoor-only and in-and-out cats have radically changed. This book was written to, hopefully, inspire friendship with these quite ordinary yet bewitching creatures. They are entitled to be as well treated as possible by their human friends. So, Mowgli, will you please get your paws off my typewriter so I can begin writing a book.

Why People Keep Cats

*Facing page:
Cats are
becoming the
most favorite
and most
numerous
domestic
animals; in
Germany, for
example, they
are estimated
at 4.5 million.
They come in a
wide variety of
colors. Only 10
to 12 percent
are pedigreed
cats.*

Within each of the developed Western countries there are at this time millions of cats, and the number is rising with each passing year. Luckily, no one pays taxes for cats—not yet! My own analysis of our society leads me to believe that we'll soon have to pay taxes on *anything* that's fun. Statistics suggest dogs are kept in homes with above-average incomes, while cats live in homes with less money. Maybe that's why dogs, not cats, need licenses?

I certainly don't like the idea of cats as just tax-savers or substitute dogs, but I'll come back to that later. On the other hand, you can say that the richer householder, in many cases, is a home owner, hence the need of a dog for security purposes. The cat should not suffer any loss in social standing...it's apparently becoming more and more the 'animal of choice' among so-called 'intellectuals.' But I wonder whether, in some cases, that really makes the cat any happier or not.

WHY ARE MORE PEOPLE KEEPING CATS?

The increasing number of pet cats is without a doubt related to the increasing number of single-occupancy households. That's definitely not a mere statistical correlation. We won't, just yet, get into whether the cats are used as companions, surrogate children, or even misused. Today, many people choose, or are forced, to live by themselves. Such existence can be very lonely but, with a cat, you have at least some form of company. The cat is in many ways a more convenient pet than a dog. You do not have to give it a walk—simply open the door and it takes itself! Also, it is less expensive to feed and is less demanding, at least in theory, on your time and attention. A cat will not tear down your door out of boredom, though it might scratch your furniture if not provided with a suitable alternative to this. It will hardly annoy your neighbors with its incessant barking, nor will it chase children and adults alike if it is not trained. Further, many landlords will not permit dogs to be kept on their premises. But they tend to be more sympathetic where cats are concerned, especially if only one or two are owned. There are thus many reasons why cats are now outnumbering dogs as a first choice pet. With the increasing number of cat owners there is the

danger that the wrong people will acquire cats for the wrong reasons. A blacklist of cat owners would include cuddlers or huggers, idolaters, and "users." Let us look at these types.

CAT CUDDLERS

The cuddlers exhibit a need to cuddle and hug something. Behavioral scientists believe that certain forms of animals trigger a brood-care drive in human beings. We know that such a drive doesn't occur in fish, snakes, lizards, or beetles. The stimuli that elicit this drive to handle an animal as if it were a human baby appear to be especially a roundish head and a soft, plushy fur that invites touching. Puppies send out these signals but later lose them as they mature into dogs that become more angular and bold in action. Cats, however, keep their soft, well-padded, cuddly kitten baby characteristics even when they grow into adults.

The cuddler is constantly stimulated to cuddle and hug. Most cats are indeed cuddly and delicate, yet the overly abundant attention of the cuddler often runs completely counter to the expectations of the poor cat. Constantly picking up a cat or smothering it in kisses and hugs robs the animal of a certain freedom, which it often seeks to protect...even with its claws. So the cuddling hugger feels rejected because his or her overbrimming love is not appreciated; such a so-called cat lover may even become a cat enemy who believes that cats are deceptive and untrustworthy beasts.

Young kittens are usually more tolerant of hugging and cuddling. There are some people, however, who somehow get rid of their growing kittens when their baby cuteness or tolerance of excessive hugging fades away. These people acquire another kitten somewhere and start hugging again. It's quite clear why I don't like this kind of cat owner.

Children are particularly prone to cuddling, which certainly does no harm to plushy toy animals. With live specimens, on the other hand, adults have to teach their children how to respect the animals. I'm not exactly an advocate of keeping cats in families with very small children. But that's not always possible when the cat was there first. In such cases, the cat and small child should be kept as far apart as possible until the child learns to respect the cat for what it is: a living animal, not a cuddly toy.

CAT IDOLATERS

While cuddlers want to be too close to their cats, idolaters want to stand off and hold them in awe as though they were icons. The idolaters often stand in the same relationship to other human beings, that is, standoffish. They feel misunderstood and often take up with cats in the mistaken belief that cats are likewise standoffish and independent of their fellow creatures.

Idolaters spin a web of mystery about the cat and use it as a sort of drug. These people see the thousand-year-old wisdom of the Egyptian cat gods in the eyes of their cats. No doubt about it, you can induce a mild state of self-hypnosis in yourself by staring into two yellow or green cat eyes, just as you do when a physician hypnotizes you by having you fix your gaze on the shiny silver tip of a ballpoint pen. But your cat doesn't like to be stared at, since it signals aggression. I never deify my cats; rather, I humanize them. I make the assumption that their needs are basically very simple. Something to eat, something to drink, a warm nook for sleeping, and that's about it...theoretically.

THE CAT "USER"

The third type of undesirable owner, the "user," has somehow come into possession of a cat—perhaps along with a farm, or brought home by a child, or left by a departing friend or neighbor. The cat is fed, watered, bedded down, and even gets a cat tray. It is let out when it wants, but no one is worried if it doesn't appear at night to be let in. It's petted from time to time, but it's not allowed to jump up on any laps...please, watch out for cashmere slacks, or silk skirts, or allergies or something! These

people freely admit that a cat is a cute animal and quite pleasant to have around, but if one day it weren't there anymore, they wouldn't replace it. Having a cat takes just a little bit more than providing it with creature comforts.

Cat "users" have nothing against cats either in or around the home, just as long as they're easy to care for. And that's one of the great misunderstandings about cats. It arises from the observation that a cat, especially when it's allowed to go outside, gets along on a minimum of food, care and attention. 'A cat takes care of itself', is heard often in those cases. 'Cats are not attached. When we went on vacation, ours stayed with the neighbors. These people simply don't realize that the poor cat was forced to put up with it.

In reality, a cat that grows up with people is just as attached to its owner as is a dog. A dog, however, audibly bewails, or at least whimpers, while a cat usually suffers silently. There's no doubt that domestic cats, over thousands of years, have developed a need for the presence and attention of their human companions. That does, however, require human imprinting of the newborn kitten. The cat fancier assumes a responsibility. He hasn't acquired merely a new hat rack or chair for his home, but a partner. This partner, however, in contrast to a human one, can adapt well to satisfy its own needs. Your cat or cats can adjust to strict order or domestic chaos, to early- or late-rising households, to human turbulence or tranquility. But what a cat always needs is attention. This is what the cat "user" invariably fails to supply.

In return they offer us something. We enjoy their graceful movements, playfulness, appearance, and

A kitten may seem shy when you first acquire it; but with time and patience, it will soon come to feel right at home.

most of all their affectionate companionship. The cat user simply does not understand that you can get out of a cat (or any other intelligent creature) only what you put in. If you put little in, you will receive little in return, so will never know what the cat could offer in respect to affection.

THE CAT-HUMAN RELATIONSHIP

A cat, even when it's asleep, relieves us of our primordial fear of loneliness. Its delicacy,

unbroken by any impetuousness, soothes our tattered nerves. It reinforces our self-esteem and sense of being needed when it turns to us, just to us, personally. Old wives' tales have it that cats don't care one way or another for people and that cats care for people only as sources of food and shelter. It is also claimed that cats love only the physical place where they live and return there even if their human family moves away. Quite the opposite is true, witness the many almost unbelievable accounts of cats that do indeed search for and find their human family.

The relationship between cat and human is more complex than merely a variation of instinctive animal behavior. That's relatively easy to explain. Behavioral scientists agree that keeping dogs and cats as domestic animals involves an infantilization, or child-like status, of the animal. In a wild cat family, a kitten is eventually treated as an adult animal, which includes being attacked by litter mates and having to compete with them for food and mating choices. It may be chased out of the group's territory; the cat's mother and especially its father are often quite unfriendly towards the cat too. You will learn later that there are cat societies in which members live on relatively friendly terms, especially on farms. But that often seems to depend upon the size and nature of the territory.

The human being who adopts a kitten slips right into a mother role and keeps it even when the kitten grows to cathood. The cat's human parent provides food, warmth (especially in bed), pleasurable stroking and petting, which remind the cat of the mother cat's soothing, rough tongue with which she licked her kittens in the first hours and days of their existence.The struggle for survival has been canceled for cats that live in human households. They don't have to constantly be on guard; the stronger partner, the human, doesn't try to survive at the cat's expense. Today,

we generally believe that the cat sees a person as a companion, just as a dog sees a person as a fellow pack member. With this companion, there are no bones of contention or reasons for any friction; they're more agreeable than disagreeable. For a cat, its human companion is somewhat of a giant denatured cat, a delightful creature. So why not be nice and loving to it?

A LIFELONG PARTNERSHIP

When I hear that, in my absence, the behavior of my cats changes and they wander restlessly through the

Nothing is more relaxed and relaxing than a peacefully sleeping cat. Watching one is enough, physicians say, to lower your blood pressure.

house, they lay down at my favorite spots, or on clothing I have worn, then I conclude that they like me personally. I'm their human friend, one that cannot be fully replaced by any other.

That's why everyone should think twice about acquiring a cat and developing such a relationship with it, because separation would mean mental or emotional, and even physical, cruelty. One becomes a cat fancier for life. And that's not any condemnation, but a calling. It's a lot of fun, and I dare say, even blissful.

A household pet of undetermined breed. Its markings are known as tortie and white.

The History of Domestic Cats

The history of the cat is laced with anecdotes and legends, hence entertaining. As far as factual history goes, it's all very vague, and scientists admit that they are left mainly with suppositions, assumptions and conjectures. We are interested in the origin and development only to the extent that they elucidate the nature and proper care of our cats. Scientists, on the other hand, no doubt get quite interested in, even excited about, whether a newly excavated skeleton from such-and-such an era thousands of years before Christ was still a wildcat, or whether it had already been domesticated and lived around the hearth of a human being's family...all of which is very hard to tell, as we'll see later.

For us normal cat buffs, it's important to know whether our cats are really domesticated or are really wild animals that live with man, as scientists have long contended. This argument of the cat's being a wild animal has often been used against keeping cats as pets in general, particularly in a home, and is supposed to elicit a guilty conscience in potential cat owners. Such opposition comes from people who want everything to be completely natural, although they live in quite unnatural, centrally heated homes, not in any forest.

Even in Grzimek's widely known book *Animal Life Encyclopedia*, we read that 'The home cat usually regards its owner not as a companion but only as some object from the cat's territory, of which the owner's home is only part; so the cat is often depicted as an untamed domestic animal.' Despite that, or perhaps because of it, there are countless numbers of cat fans in the

Felis silvestris silvestris, the European wildcat. It is untameable. Our cuddly house cats are, so to say, its cousins.

world. Ever since the first appearance of the Egyptian temple cats, man has loved the unadulterated wild animal in them. We even maintain that our house cat helps us by catching mice, but in reality most cat owners keep cats out of pure enjoyment. We enjoy the company of a playful, highly sensitive animal that has not become our utter slave but has kept its independence, even under our daily care.

All of the above is a completely antiquated idea. It has since come to light that cats behave toward people just the way they do toward their own kind. They wouldn't ever carry on like that with a tree or some other object from their territory. In addition, cats have developed still other means of communication which they reserve exclusively for us.

Just how our cats would behave if they were indeed still genuine wild animals becomes painfully evident to those people who attempt to keep real wildcats, such as the European wildcat *Felis silvestris silvestris*, which is really untamable even if acquired as a young kitten.

EARLY DOMESTICATION

Over the thousands of years since cat first came to man, cats have exhibited a new, inherited, or learned quality that appears to make an association with humans both desirable and beneficial.Today, it's believed that this could well be the case...as long as man had

domesticated himself first and settled into a sedentary way of life. A nomadic group of people, on the other hand, certainly did not offer any home for a territorial animal like the cat. Then came along that pack-oriented animal, the ubiquitous dog, to whom it didn't make any difference at all where his pack wandered, as long as a warming hearth and edible remnants of the hunt were available.

The question of when the first domestic cats appeared is usually answered by the ordinary person as in ancient Egypt, whereby is meant something vaguely associated with pyramids and pharaohs. One doesn't realize that thousands of years embrace this early civilization. In essence, however, the answer is right. The first documented appearance of the domestic cat was in the civilization of the Egyptians.

There is also evidence that cats shared other civilizations and cultures with man. Statuettes have been unearthed in Anatolia which depict women playing with cats, and even nursing them. These finds were from the sixth century B.C., and it can hardly be assumed that women tried that with wildcats. Excavations in Jericho, too, revealed cat skeletons buried in the layers associated with human dwellings; it's not completely certain, however, that they hadn't been hunted merely for food or fur.

THE PROBABLE PROCESS OF DOMESTICATION

The first inscriptions and drawings dealing with cats appeared in Egypt about 2000 B.C. "Mau" is the name reported, but that's doubtlessly an onomatopoeic name. Interestingly, cats are "mao" in Chinese. What kinds of cats were the ones that the Egyptians adopted...or vice versa? We now mostly agree that it was *Felis silvestris libyca,* the Nubian pale yellow cat, a subspecies of *Felis silvestris silvestris,* the European wildcat. Wildcats and domestic cats hardly differ structurally from one another. And, as already mentioned, that's just what makes it so hard to classify finds. In contrast to the European wildcat, the sandy- or dun-colored subspecies of Africa is more lithe and high-legged, with its color almost matching that of the sand. In addition, there were also lightly speckled and variously marked kinds. *Felis s. libyca,* above all, felt attracted to humankind. Cats like it are still being caught wild in Africa, in Kenya for example. When these cats are captured young, they can usually be brought up as domestic house cats.

The teaming up of cat and man in ancient Egypt could have occurred much as it does in Kenya. Egyptian culture arose, as is well known, because people in the Nile valley discovered the secret of artificial irrigation, leading to abundant harvests. The food surplus was stored in huge granaries...to the ecstatic joy of man's first cultural hangers-on, rats and mice. And this was also a joy to all the cats that suddenly discovered this catfood paradise on the rim of their rather frugal steppes. It's easy to imagine how they first merely raided this land of plenty then later comfortably settled in closer. The Egyptians would have been rather stupid not to have quickly recognized the value of these new immigrants from the desert steppes.

James A. Serpell, the British scientist who dealt especially with this matter, didn't believe the Egyptians were passive bystanders who merely tolerated the cats. He tells us that the peoples of the most ancient dynasties of the Nile showed a marked passion for keeping and taming animals, which included monkeys, baboons, hyenas, mongooses, crocodiles, and even lions. Serpell thinks that an animal as charming as the cat would have won the hearts of the Egyptians and been taken into their homes even without any demonstration of their usefulness in annihilating rodents. All these animals were more or less deified and revered, well fed and spoiled, probably the residue of an old belief in totems. Any cats that responded well to this good treatment were no doubt kept as pets, thus leading to domesticated lines of clearly less timid individuals who became friendly even toward man.

THE EGYPTIAN CAT CULTS

That cats were deified is seen in an anecdote provided by the writer Axel Eggebrecht. Whether he discovered it somewhere or invented it is unimportant. The story goes like this: The lion goddess in Egypt was named Boast, or Bastet. She had her own city, Bubastis. The people demanded a physical presence of the divine animal. The Bastet priests, unlike their colleagues who served Apisstier, had a more difficult task because the lion was more of an inconvenient cult object that often took his divinity seriously and breakfasted on his priestly servants instead of letting himself be adored by them.

At that time, about 2500 B.C., a clever Bastet, or lion priest, went on expedition into Nubia to find new animal divinities to import. There he saw a small sandy-yellowish animal that looked deceptively similar to a lion cub but was gentler, easy to stroke and even pick up to carry.

The clever Bastet priest took one of these remarkable animals home to Egypt with him and presented it at the next general synod; all of his colleagues were thrilled, and thereupon the inconvenient lion was speedily replaced by this smaller, more practical animal. Not only Bastet was represented with a cat's head: there were other cat divinities in the pantheon of the Egyptians. The god Ra took on cat form in his battle with the serpent of evil, just like Isis, and even Osiris.

The puzzling eye glow of cats, which varies according to the lights, was equated with the waxing and waning of the moon, as well as with the sun's position. Since these natural events were of utmost importance to the agricultural planning of the Egyptians, cat magic was in demand. The importance of the Bastet cult grew over the centuries, reaching its zenith in the last thousand years before Christ.The usually reliable chronicler Herodotus reported on the great festivities in Bubastis during April and May, at which up to 700,000 people are supposed to have participated. Bubastis had grandiose temples and cat statues, cat statuettes and cat relief sculptures. Great amounts of alcohol were consumed at orgies which smacked of savage feline libido.

Cat reproduction, however, continued according to the natural cycles of their ancestors. One inscription reported that a cat had twenty-eight kittens in seven years, something that was considered worthy of mention. In this regard, Herodotus writes that the Egyptian tomcats applied a drastic remedy so that they could engage in more frequent sex: they dragged off any unguarded kittens and killed them but didn't eat them. The female, once her kittens were gone, was ready to mate again. Is this an ancestral memory in the collective subconscious of all cat mothers that makes them particularly quick-tempered against even an ordinarily familiar tomcat?

Cats were by no means in excess, and they were expensive. The number of cats in the household determined that home's status. When a house cat died, all the members of the household shaved their eyebrows off and mourned until they grew back. Wealthy people had their cats

cat fled for their lives so as not to be associated with the body. About 50 B.C., the Roman writer Diodorus reported a full-scale rebellion because a Roman soldier had killed a cat. The Roman authorities couldn't or wouldn't keep the mob from lynching the perpetrator.

Since cats were as expensive as holy, the Egyptians tried by all means to prevent their export to other countries. They even

embalmed and buried along with costly gifts, including dead mice, in special cat cemeteries. In Bubastis were found burial sites which contained thousands of cat mummies, of which a portion has been irreverently exhumed and shipped to England to be spread as agricultural fertilizer! Outbreaks of religious fanaticism have occurred over cats. Killing a cat brought corporal and capital punishment; it went so far that people who found a dead

had a sort of intelligence service to seek out cats abroad that had been smuggled out of the country and either buy them back or kidnap and repatriate them.

The Egyptians mysterious doings and claims to exclusivity only aroused their neighbors' covetousness. We assume that it was the wily, shrewd Phoenicians, those international merchants of the time, who took cats out of Egypt back to their home ports. The Phoenicians apparently had nothing better

All young kittens need frequent physical contact with their mother. The cat owner can utilize this need and replace the mama cat.

to do than have these cats symbolize their rather promiscuous love goddess Astarte. This unfortunate association was to have an unhappy effect on cats later on in history.

HOW CATS SPREAD AROUND THE WORLD

Because the cat is a rather problem-free seafarer, it transported well on Phoenician ships to Italy and Greece, probably first to Greece, and then along with Greek colonization into southern Italy. Greeks and Romans didn't know at first just what to do with cats, for these people already kept polecats (fitchets, or ferrets, as we know them today) as well as snakes to catch their mice. Cats became exotic or ornamental pets in affluent households, something like parrots and monkeys today.

Germanic farmers kept weasels at home to catch mice, though cats were certainly known from early times because of the Roman occupation and trade with them. Even during pagan times, for example, cats drew the carriage of the Nordic goddess Freya.

Freya, like Astarte earlier, was also involved with reproduction and its related sexual activities, so this, too, was to augur poorly for cats once the early Middle Ages rolled around. But before that bad luck was to come upon the cat, it still had a career not as mouser, but as rat catcher. Rats appeared in large numbers about the time

of the great migrations of the Vandals, Huns, and Goths through central Europe. The usual small animals the peasants and urban folk kept for catching mice couldn't do the job adequately. So, for several hundred years, the cat was a highly valued household member and no doubt also a crew member of ships. That's probably how it reached the rest of the world, though it most likely underwent a secondary domestication in some places. It almost certainly participated in crosses with other cat species and varieties over the course of time.

OLD EUROPE: THE CAT'S DARK AGES

The really dark ages for cats began in Europe. Religious fanaticism raised its ugly head ominously about the year 100 A.D. That was about the time the world was expected to end, and the growing power of the Church directed itself mainly against the remnants of the old superstitions, regardless of whether they were Germanic or pagan Roman. The cat must have had to pay dearly for its erstwhile association with the old mother earth and fertility divinities.

Beginning with the 12th century, it was equated with demons and was a symbol of heresy, associated with all the grimly annihilated sects such as the Waldenses, Albigenses and Templars. The ecclesiastical authorities described the feasts of the

faithful as wild orgies presided over by cats, or one huge one. A typical token of submission to Satan was supposed to be kissing the cat's anus.

To this mystique also belonged herbalists and healers, as well as runic inscription interpreters, all usually women, who often kept cats, perhaps only to protect their stores of herbs from rodents. These women were soon seen as witches, and for many centuries cats and witches were almost synonymous. Cats supposedly had to be killed before they reached twenty years of age, otherwise they would be transformed into witches; and once such a witch became one hundred years old, she would be turned right back into a cat. There was scarcely any witch trial in which a cat didn't figure, either as co-defendant or as accomplice; as a result, the cat was condemned and burned along with the witch.

Hate for cats was possibly a reflection of the church's attitude toward women, who were the ones who tempted man away from chastity, the lofty ultimate goal. They were sensual, delicate, challengingly receptive then coquettishly standoffish, unpredictable, even unfaithful. Didn't that all go with a cat's personality and nature? And wasn't it significant that precisely in the country where witch-hunting raged the most horrendously, in Germany, the word *katze*, meaning cat, referred to witches? That didn't happen, for example, to the luckier French pussycat, *le* (the—masculine) *chat*. No, just the German *katze* symbolized everything corrupt and evil about woman.

Adulteresses were drowned in a sack along with a live cat, this practice also being used for unfaithful wives in Turkey. Holiday activities involved driving out the devil and evil temptations, along with cat hunts and killing. When a cat didn't just simply die after being beaten or thrown off a roof, for example, that was proof enough that it was in league with the devil. And that's why cats just had to be doing bad things. In the *Handbook of German Superstitions*, over eighteen columns of text are dedicated to the evils of cats, like snatching the air away from babies and causing epidemics because they licked toads and polluted drinking water. Even a cat's cough was enough to sour a marriage. They served as scapegoats for every and all ills. That, paradoxically, may have even assured their survival. If cats were indeed troublemakers and so strongly evil, then perhaps a saucer of milk could bribe them into allowing themselves to be used as magic against even worse demons. In some places it became customary to first send a black cat into a newly built house to draw off, so as to speak, any evil in it. All cats were believed to be evil, and the black ones worst of all, though in some localities, such as in Yorkshire, England, colors were reversed, and it was the white ones which were regarded as the most evil. These superstitions are still around today. That's why, years ago, I got a good deal on my ebony-black cat Ophelia. She sat in a large cage in the

A Somali kitten playfully swiping at a ball of yarn. Cats are clever animals and can easily amuse themselves.

window of a pet shop in Hamburg, Germany, along with six or seven normal Siamese cats. These were apparently sold quite quickly, leaving only Ophelia sitting in the large cage. Her constant joyousness won my heart and I decided to purchase her. They gave her to me for next to nothing because no one wants a black cat! Ophelia has been one of the most charming (even bewitching!) cats I've ever known. The merciless annihilation of cats during the Middle Ages had a sort of macabre effect, according to many historians. In the wake of the Crusades, migratory rats invaded Europe, bringing the plague organisms in their fleas. The great epidemic of this plague, known as the Black Death, which literally decimated wide expanses of the European continent, would have been significantly less grim had there been more cats around!

THE SWING BACK TO CAT POPULARITY

Ordinary common sense surfaced first among the farmers, who could plainly see just how useful cats were every day on the farms. It was on the farms that cats survived these anti-cat years; cats weren't particularly loved on farms but were at least tolerated, just as they still are today. The blossoming period of the Renaissance in Europe reintroduced cats into the cities, dwellings and even into boudoirs and salons. Cats were fashionable too, from time to time, at the French court, no doubt due to the influence of Cardinal Richelieu, who liked to work surrounded by kittens and left a sum of money for their upkeep after his death.

The voyage of discovery to the New World opened up new habitats to cats. Again, they came as crew members on rat-infested sailing ships, where their services were indispensable. Now that more is known of genetics, we can prove that in certain instances cat lines which descended from cats of the voyagers' home ports back in Europe remained dominant where they first settled in the New World. Though the cat has survived and done well enough, its reputation hasn't always been the best. Up until the nineteenth century, serious scholars were classifying animals into good and bad ones, based upon supposed possession or lack of character. From that time we still have residual prejudices that the cat is allegedly false, uninterested in people, unfaithful, and interested only in the physical home. This merely underlines the fact that for all the knowledge we humans gained over the centuries, we still remained very ignorant organisms until very recent times. Indeed, prejudices still exist in the minds of many people. They are passed from one generation to the next.

Moggie or Purebred Cat?

One's own cat is always the prettiest. And that's going to be true even at the end of this chapter. Besides being the prettiest, most beautiful, and most intelligent, your own cat is also the friendliest and most personable ever reported...these being obvious facts to any true cat fancier. For people who have once had the perfect cat or cats, we can hardly dissuade them from loving any others; this book, however, is for relatively new cat fanciers, so we'll try to give a broad picture of just what is on the cat market these days.

There is a chance that your first search for a kitten will lead to the ordinary house cat, affectionately known as a moggie, meaning a cat of no particular breeding. About 80 to 90% of the millions of cats living with humans are in fact moggies. The rest are specific breeds or mixtures of them.

THE TYPICAL MOGGIE HOUSE CAT

The normal house cat is a grayish-black, speckled, or tiger-like tabby, and even this latter kind hardly appears any more in its pure form, unless specifically bred for this. Most are grayish-black with one or more white paws, white on the chest, black or white facial areas, and brownish or yellowish markings here and there. Then there's the whole array of house cats in other colors: black, white, black-and-white, tortoiseshell, and many others, including that most ubiquitous of family cats: the famous ginger, who often turns out to be a tom!

All of this variety can be explained quite scientifically with the concepts of dominant and recessive genes and the ever increasingly better understanding of the laws of heredity. But I won't bore you with all that science, except to note that not only color can vary but also body and head shape, kind of fur, and many other characteristics can vary. A cat can have a large round or a small pointed head, depending upon whether a Persian, Russian Blue or Siamese might have gotten into the ancestry somewhere along the line. Then there are also leggy cats and those which are cobby and squat. The fur can be shorthaired, medium, or longhaired, and weight can vary greatly from barely eight pounds to twenty-five pounds (the latter weight for a very large or fat cat).

House cats, in some countries, may also crossbreed with native wild species of cat, though according to reports a stray house cat would most likely be eaten instead of being mated. If a stray house cat were to actually fertilize a wild female, the offering would hardly come to the attention of humans.

In a nutshell, the house cat is very variable, this extending to its nature. Mother cats sometimes become that way by chance, not by any intentional breeding plans. It is quite possible, indeed even probable, that a darling little dear has been at it with the most roughneck tom in the neighborhood. It can show quite plainly in the offspring. With specific breeds, however, you can anticipate just how the next generation will look; variation is minimal if the mating is according to breed standards. Reference books amply describe colors and markings, kinds of fur, and head forms that the expectant mother can be expected to deliver.

The question of character and personality, however, is still rather unresolved, even for experts. Nevertheless, predictions are still attempted—temperamental, calm, playful, vocal, enterprising, and so on. Experts, however, carefully add the words 'normally or usually' to qualify their subjective opinions. Individual differences even within the same breed can be enormous.

When I obtained my first Siamese Mao, I asked an expert if I could let him run free without the risk of the local common cats tearing him up. 'Tear him up?' the expert said. You might just as well let a tiger loose…worry about the neighbor's cats!' In reality, Mao came back from his first encounter with the neighbors' cats as a confirmed pacifist; from then on he simply fled away from any quarrelsome cats.

By contrast, the English writer Joyce Stranger reported that her Siamese male Kym had been the greatest fighter in the neighborhood, which cost her many hours of nursing and visits to the vet. Frankly, I preferred my Mao.

Considering all of that possible variety, even in specific breeds, I can tell you only very little about what to expect from your new cat. The kitten's mother and the household into which the kitten is born make definite impressions upon it during its first weeks of life. Thereafter, its entire personality will be greatly influenced by its new owner, the environment in which it lives, and the way it is reared.

THE BREED CRAZE

A number of breeds have been around over 100 years in their present, precisely defined form. Cat-loving England laid the groundwork in 1871 with the first cat show, which was soon followed by a rash of clubs and associations. Standards for each breed were established, as well as guidelines for judges, who thereupon bestowed magnificently sounding titles like Champion and International Champion on the winners. German clubs, for example, followed a certain Professor Schwangartner's efforts to establish the rules.

None of that is very important to the *average* cat lover. If you really want a specific breed, make sure you research it very carefully before you make your purchase. Most breeders won't encourage you to breed your own cat, unless it's especially rare or especially handsome. Be advised that if you want to breed your own cats, you must join a club and exhibit them at shows in order to gain recognition and maybe illustrious titles for your winners.

Personally, I find all that show business taxing for human and cat alike. This sort of activity attracts the most common variety of club joiner and, to some extent, generates professional jealousy (the increasing interest in cats has given the breeder's art more of a money smell). I know several breeders who have left all that behind and now breed cats only for their own enjoyment and that of their clientele. This said, were it

not for the cat shows and those who participate in them, there would be far less breeds to choose from. Indeed, without the show side of the hobby, there would hardly be breeds in the modern sense at all, and this book's potential market would be greatly diminished!

So, personal views aside, let's make a little survey of cat breeds. I won't go too much into details about colors or markings but

The CAT-A-LAC from Designer Products, Inc. A travel case such as this is ideal for transporting your pet.

will try to give you an idea of how your cat will look when grown and what behavior you might generally expect from it. Again, realize that cats can turn out quite differently than expected. Logically, it seems best to start with the shorthaired cats, then go on to the longhairs, and finally the semi-longhairs.

SHORTHAIRED CATS

The shorthaired breeds, even as far back as the first domestics of Egypt, are the most natural cats. Breeding some of them, however, can create problems. A case in point is the Manx, a tailless cat. It was bred by accident and, for unknown reasons, continued to be bred on the English Isle of Man. Taillessness is unfortunately related to internal malformation. Breeding many cats can be associated with serious complications. Manx breeders must be diligent in their efforts to prevent vetebral malformation.

EUROPEAN AND AMERICAN SHORTHAIRED CATS

European shorthaired cats are practical house cats that have been improved somewhat through breeding. Some Persian has been bred in to get a somewhat heavier build than the usual house cat possesses; also, very attractive and bright coloration has been developed. For a time, cats of only one color were preferred: black, white, cream, and blue. Then there is the two-tone combination blue-cream, the three-tone tortoiseshell (of black, red and cream), and the four-tone (tortoiseshell plus white). Also, there are the usual colorations and markings of the traditionally gray-speckled house cat.

The most beautiful part of all this is that all these colors also pop up spontaneously in ordinary cats...some of these moggie cats even winning prizes at shows in special classes. Their house cat ancestry has given domestic purebred cats their robust nature as well as their spirit. You can expect from them just what you can from a house cat, but they do tend to wander less than, say, a farm cat. In my opinion, though, that's due more to how they were raised; people take more care of them, for, after all, they are thoroughbreds. A cat about which people care a lot, cares a lot about people.

SIAMESE CATS

In my opinion, the breeding of what was a very elegant feline has been overdone. The wedge-like head was bred longer and longer and the body build made more delicate. The specimens I've seen at recent cat shows reminded me of Walt Disney's Bambi but with his ears cropped. They look as if they even have to be protected from a wind which would otherwise sweep them away. I can't really say what caused this breeding trend in Siamese. It hasn't improved the breed. In Europe, there seems to be a change in trend now. Old-fashioned friends of this breed are now getting robust individuals again by importing examples from countries where the old type is still seen. The history of the Siamese cat shows that this overdoing of the breed contradicts the essence of the breed. They actually originated in Siam (now called Thailand), presumably as a mutation from the Egyptian Mau, and have been documented and depicted from the 14th century. They are marked with the characteristic facial mask and points but the head is significantly rounder than those of today, even though the pronounced muzzle is quite recognizable. There's no doubt that the Siamese cats were palace and temple cats. Besides these cats, there were, and still are, other kinds of cats for the simple folk.

It is thought that the first Siamese cats were brought to Europe in 1884 by a retiring British general consul, to whom they were presented personally by the king of Siam. However, Siamese cats appeared at the first cat show in London in 1871. People described their appearance as lemur-like and nightmare cats, again the old association with the devil.

In older literature, the body build of the Siamese is described as slender, but muscular, and elegant. Today, because of the comments I have drawn attention to, I'd personally call the Siamese frail.

And that's a shame, for what is fascinating about the Siamese cat is its nature. No other cat is more attracted to man. Many people have called them the most dog-like cat, which is an unfortunate comparison, in my opinion. The fact remains, the Siamese cat will drop everything when its human companion appears. It quickly adapts to the human life style. It is always alert and ready to be spoken to, or to speak at any time. And how it can speak! The Siamese cat possesses an

Siamese cats are the basis for several other breeds, such as the Burmese. Burmese cats, which come in a number of colors, have a somewhat quieter disposition than do Siamese.

extraordinarily rich vocabulary with which to express itself, be it of hunger, love, fear, complaint, and even boredom. On the other hand, there's certainly no boredom for the human companion of a Siamese cat, which turns out to be an ever ready partner for conversation, stroking and games...all of which gets you involved in an endless round of activities. The original Siamese color is sealpoint, a dark brown, but other colors have been developed. They include chocolate, blue, lilac and many more.

BURMESE AND HAVANA CATS

The Siamese is the ancestor of a number of breeds, the Burmese and Havana being two of them. They are considered to be bringers of good luck in the Far East. Burmese cats come in a limited color range, of which brown is the most

The Havana was also derived from the Siamese. It was purposely bred from Siamese and various one-color cats; the coat should be a rich chestnut brown.

numerous colors, as well as speckled or stippled and spotted. The black ones are especially impressive because they resemble black panthers.

The color blue is considered lucky, or at least protection against spirits, in many cultures (hence the blue house walls and ocular symbols in the Mediterranean area). No wonder that blue cats were highly valued. Four breeds today have this fur color: the Chartreux, the Russian and British Blues, and the Korat, the latter being of mildly foreign type as would be expected of a breed from Thailand (formerly Siam).

popular, with the Siamese markings still faintly apparent. Their owners describe their character as that of Siamese with throttled-down steam, meaning lively but not with the full-steam frenzy that sometimes characterizes the Siamese. The Havana is slimmer than the Burmese and has a longer head. The color should be a genuine chestnut brown. It was quite purposefully bred from Siamese and one color cats. They are also said to have a modulated Siamese temperament.

ORIENTAL SHORTHAIRED CATS

Cats of the Siamese type in body build but without the accepted colors of the Siamese markings are called Foreign, Oriental or Colorpoint Shorthairs. They come in

CHARTREUX

These are really blue European shorthaired cats that have been fixed as a breed. Their standard calls for their being completely of one color, with blue lips and rose-taupe soles. Body build has to be robust and the head thick and round. They are calm, markedly delicate yet robust, and a joy to look at. One can well imagine that these cats, as the legend tells us, accompanied the silent monks who bred them and for whom they chased away the mice from their frugal storage supplies of food. Rarely, the Chartreux give birth to albinos, whose orange-yellow eyes are strikingly distinctive.

RUSSIAN BLUE

The second blue cat, the Russian blue, is steeped in legends. This breed differs from the Chartreux because of its slimmer body and green eyes. In Russia, it was supposed to have been bred and also exported for its fur. The Russian blue was once called the Archangel cat, for the Russian polar port of the same name. Its thick, heavy fur reveals its northern origin, from where it disembarked as a crew member on ships bound for western lands. The nature of the breed is calm and playful.

BRITISH BLUE

Of stocky build, this long established breed has been developed to a high standard of excellence in its homeland. It is thought to have contributed to the Chartreux gene pool when the latter breed was decimated during World War II. The source of its blue color is not known for sure and may have come via the Russian blue. It has a gentle and quiet nature.

EGYPTIAN MAU

The dream of all cat lovers was always to breed a cat that comes closest to looking like the Egyptian Mau, as we know it from the ancient descriptions. Now, a breed look- alike is available. A pair was discovered in Egypt and exported to America. After they were bred awhile, it was found that the breed had remained stable. For mystics, it must be fascinating that they are marked with an "M" on the forehead. As if in memory of the friendly Egyptians, the Mau is an exceptionally friendly cat toward people. It's leopard spots and black tail rings make it a ravishing beauty. It also has an excellent character, lively and very devoted. Maus are growing in popularity.

ABYSSINIANS

The Mau's close relative, the Abyssinian, is just as

The Oriental Shorthaired cats also have a Siamese form. Here's a black one called ebony.

attractive. It calls to mind the legend that the Egyptians brought cats from Ethiopia as replacements for lions. Well, the Abyssinians do really come from Ethiopia and were supposed to have been taken to England by a British officer returning from an expeditionary force. The color of the fur is like a hare's, which is why the French call it a hare cat. This color is called sorrel, and the pattern is actually a form of tabby. It is one of only two breeds which sport a ticked coated (the other being the Singapura). The Abyssinian has an Oriental pointed head and huge ears, often with tufts—of hair, or brushes, on them like a lynx. The body is moderately sized and high-legged. They are excellent climbers. By nature they are alert, endearing, and sensitive.

REX CATS

Rex cats are another story. Their fur is waved or wavy, like a young lamb, because the Rex coat lacks guard hairs. This mutant occurred in England in a farm cat. The effect of the mutation was also that the appearance of the cat changed; and it looked like an oriental breed, which it does to this day. It is often called 'elfish,' a rather apt description. The wavy fur is very thin, so Rex cats have to be kept warm and are easily chilled if they go out during wet weather. There are two popular Rex breeds: the Devon and the Cornish. They are separate mutations.

Ironically they were produced in neighboring counties, for whom they are named.

LONGHAIRED CATS

Long hair in cats is the result of a recessive mutation that probably appeared during the 16th century. It gave a new dimension to cat breeds because it means that all shorthaired cats can be produced in a longhaired form. Many have, and new breeds are always being developed by introducing the longhair gene into shorthaired breeds.Unless you are one of those people who really enjoy grooming, it is best to admire longhairs rather than own them. Their fur quickly picks up thorns, grasses, small twigs and all manner of other bits and pieces. When wet, they look very bedraggled, and if the coat is allowed to become matted, this may necessitate using scissors to cut the mats off. Longhaired cats also lick their fur constantly and may swallow so much that it forms hairballs that can create minor blockages in their digestive systems. But this is usually restricted to the Persian breed, other longhairs not being such a problem. Some longhaired breeds, such as the Somali (longhaired Abyssinian) or the Balinese (longhaired Siamese), have much more manageable fur, so are ideal for the person looking for a breed needing only a regular, rather than dedicated, grooming. It's often said that the longhaired cats are more

Persian. This elegant breed maintains a prestigious position in the world of cats. The crowning glory of the Persian is its long flowing coat.

domestic and less temperamental than others, but this is not so for most breeds. But it may be so for the Persian, which has been bred in greater numbers than any other breed. Constant selection for a mild nature has produced a breed that is often a stay-at-home and which has its feline traits diluted to a greater degree than any other breed. This is the best breed for anyone who wants a really calm cat that does a lot of staying put.

PERSIANS

Persians are very impressive cats (depending on your taste in felines), and it often wins the Best in Show award at the large cat exhibitions. They are large and massive in their build, but their long fur makes them appear larger than they really are. The head is round and broad, with large round eyes. They have a pug- or snub-nosed sort of look to them—some would call it aloofness or inscrutability. But the breed standard calls for it. The little ears almost disappear into the desirable ruffled neck frill. Persian cats often have problems giving birth because of their newborns' large heads. The flattened noses often create breathing problems in warm weather. There is thus a price to be paid to owning one of these top show breeds. Persians come in all colors and with various eye shades.

Mixed-breed kittens. A pair of kittens can be great friends and companions for each other.

Bicolor and tricolor Persian cats are recognized, and you can have tabby Persians as well.

ANGORA AND VAN CATS

Many years ago there was little or no distinction between the Angora of Turkey and the Persian. They were often freely bred to each other and the result was the modern Persian with its profuse coat, which the original Persians didn't have. The Angora faded into obscurity but was maintained in its homeland. It is now a breed of growing popularity. It most likely arrived in Europe as early as the 16th century. Cardinal Richelieu's cats were supposed to have been Angoras. Angoras have a longer and more obviously feline head than the Persian. Their fur is long and silky without being dense like the Persian. There are many color shades, but the pure white ones were thought to be the original genuine article. However, this is not so. It is the length and texture of the coat that is the hallmark of being Angora, not its color. I was fascinated when I recently saw one of the first ones to appear in Germany. The Angoras are apparently much more enterprising than Persians, and hence much more pampered and attached to their human companions. The completely snow white Angoras are said to be deaf more often than others are, but cats can compensate for that with other senses.

The Van breed, certainly related to Angoras, is named for Lake Van in Turkey. There is an interesting peculiarity with this breed. Though all cats can swim in emergencies, they usually shy away from water, but the Van cats swim in the brackish waters of Lake Van and in other bodies of water too. Vans are white, except for auburn markings on head and tail. The true Van of Turkey is actually an all-white, odd-eyed cat (meaning each eye is of a different color), but the Western Van breed is associated with the colored markings, and this became the form around which the standard was drafted.

COLORPOINT LONGHAIRS

There has never been any lack of attempts to breed somewhat more pep into

Persians without losing their impressive looks. One of these successful attempts produced Colorpoint Longhairs, also known as Himalayans. The Siamese was mated with Persians to produce a breed with Persian looks but with Siamese markings. Once the Siamese type was bred out of the new colorpoint cats they became totally Persian in their looks. Today, many associations regard the Himalayan as just another color variety of the Persian. It displays the same character as the Persian, though some owners insist that these cats do still have a mischievous hint of Siamese in them.

BIRMAN

In France, the Birman is called *Chat Sacre Du Birmanie*, the sacred cat of Burma. At first, this was believed to be a breeder's trick to sell crosses of Siamese with pure whites for a good price. Stories were circulated that the people rose in protest against the exportation of their holy temple cats. Later, people

Birman. Longhaired breeds such as this will need regular grooming to keep them looking their best.

began thinking that there indeed could be a grain of truth in the stories. An accidental cross could have occurred long ago in this ancient kingdom, which produced a cat whose mysterious air led to its adoption by Buddhist priests.

There's a legend that goes: During an attack on a monastery, the pure-white ancestral mother of the Burmese cat is supposed to have sat on the body of a massacred priest at the very moment when the temple goddess shot electrifying bolts of vengeance from her sapphire-blue eyes that zapped the assailants. All his dazzling power gave the Birman its dark markings and light blue eyes, leaving only its paws, resting on the martyr's body, pure white. The coat of the Birman is dense without being as profuse as that of a Persian. It has an endearing nature— being quiet—yet is full of the joys of life. The breed is 'pointed' without being totally so. The face, ears, tail and legs are darker in color than the body, the feet being white—a feature of this breed. You can have a Birman in seal, blue, chocolate or lilac, and other colors are being developed.

NORWEGIAN FOREST AND MAINE COON CATS

The Norwegian Forest and Maine Coon breeds will appeal to those who like a cat that resembles the wildcat of Europe. The two breeds are so similar in looks and temperament that the average person can't tell them apart.

The Norwegian Forest is an ancient breed that was mentioned in the Scandinavian sagas. Over the course of centuries, it has adapted to the inhospitable conditions of northern Europe by developing a soft, insulating underfur and, as a raincoat above it, a tough, water repellent outer coat. A neck ruffle nicely frames a clear cut, rather full cat head. This cat is a good climber and hunter, yet it is thoroughly at home in its owner's house. In the sparsely settled regions of Norway, the Forest cat is obviously largely an outside cat. That is less so in the case of the Maine Coon. It looks very much like the Forest cat but is larger. Some Maine Coon cats grow into the largest domestic cats that there are, with the exception of the Siberian, a new breed in the West. They may weight up to twenty pounds (or more if overfed).

The Maine Coon is from Maine, the northeastern USA state for which it is named. People once thought it was the offspring of a cat and a raccoon, but this is genetically impossible. It is available in very many colors and tabby coat patterns. It well may be that its origins lie in Norway, from whence it was taken by early emigrants. But it is also possible that it is the result of hybridization between early Angoras and Persians with local American shorthairs. Once the longhair gene was transposed, the resulting cats would breed true if mated to other longhairs. The harsh conditions of the Maine winters would certainly have been a 'make or break' situation for the cats that survived, so the result is a very hardy breed that after a severe decline some years ago is now returning to popularity in large numbers.

MEDIUM COATED LONGHAIRED CATS

The recessive gene that creates long hair in cats does not always do so in the same way within every breed. For example, the Somali and the Balinese both sport long coats, but they are not of the dense type seen in the Persian. However, the original Persian was not like the breed of today, so breeder selection for a more dense coat is a factor in controlling density. The result of these realities is that there are a number of breeds which display a coat that is either long and silky, though not especially dense, or is dense but not especially long. There is no official group for such breeds because in show classifications, a breed either has a short coat or a long one, of whatever type the latter is. But as a first-time owner, it is useful for you to know that these medium-coated breeds do exist and represent a compromise for those who would like a longish coated cat without it being of the Persian or Maine Coon type.

Examples, apart from those cited, are the Ragdoll, an American breed gaining in popularity, the Exotic Shorthair, which is the hybrid of the Persian and the American Shorthair, the Nebelung, which is a longhaired Russian Blue, and the Cymric, which is a longhaired Manx. In the foregoing look at the cat breeds, I have described only a few of those that you can select from. This book is essentially about cats as living companions rather than being a full survey of the many breeds now available, But those mentioned represent some of the most popular breeds, and a few that are more rarely seen. If you wish to read all about every breed, then I advise you to purchase *The Atlas of Cats of the World* by Dennis Kelsey-Wood, which describes them all and indicates the many colors in which each is available.

The Chartreux is really supposed to have been bred by the silent Carthusian monks. The coat is blue, which is considered by many cultures to bring luck and happiness.

Selecting a Cat or Kitten

In deciding to become a cat owner or, more appropriately, having elected to live with a cat, I do hope you have considered well that you will be assuming responsibility for a sensitive creature that may well live for 20 or more years—barring accidents or a fatal disease.

How do you find an animal that you'll really enjoy? Basically, it's often enough to decide 'I want a cat!' It's like that well-known coincidence that the moment you start talking about something you want, someone pedals one right to you. Once you become interested in cats, you suddenly begin seeing them all over the place. They show up at the neighbor's house and garden, where you've never consciously seen them before. You remember all at once that someone you once knew always talked about cats, that your Aunt Lily had cats all her life, that your fellow office employee has her bulletin board smothered in cat pictures, ostensibly her own (since she's shown cuddling most of them).

It's worth the time and effort, as a first step, to glance around at these surroundings where cats happily reside. It's not the worst start to choose a kitten from the litter of a neighbor's cat.

First, watch discreetly how the neighbor's cat is enjoying life, how it's fed and generally cared for. Second, as the professed animal lover that you are, keep track of the kittens during their first weeks but without committing yourself yet to any choice. Third, the neighbor (if we're talking about purebred cats, which today represent some expense) will show a natural timidity about prices, which, by contrast, cat breeders often lose when dealing with total strangers.

BEWARE OF GIFT CATS

It is possible, of course, to receive a cat for free, though that can cost a great deal under certain circumstances. You've got to look a gift cat in the mouth, and everywhere else too! That will save you unpleasant surprises and vet bills later. I'll tell you what to watch for when we get to buying a cat.

Gift cats can be a problem. The very fact that someone is ready to give kittens away shows that they haven't taken proper care of the mother cat. If the cat owner planned for the mother to have kittens without first arranging for happy homes for them, then this indicates a certain irresponsibility that possibly also continues

during the kittens' critical first weeks of life, leading to various problems.

If the mother's pregnancy was unwanted, it probably happened during her first year, and that's not a good beginning for quality offspring. If the mother was an older cat, then any responsible animal lover would have had her spayed. An owner like that realizes the misery associated with the unlimited propagation of alley and other wandering cats. If not, then they haven't thought very much about their cat, and are therefore not the ideal source of a new kitten.

Still...you can also find healthy, attractive and friendly kittens from those sources if you carefully observe the surroundings and behavior of the youngsters.

A LITTLE ABOUT STRAYS

The same applies to taking in a stray cat, in which case the adoption is often really of *you* by the *cat!* Unfortunately, however, there are still far too many homeless cats wandering about. Nature romantics think such a free-ranging life must be heaven

for cats. The cats, however, think quite differently. They more likely know how to appreciate the punctuality of mealtimes and the security of a human home. It's very moving to see how such cats, which have definitely not had the best experience at the hands of human beings, really throw themselves on you if you care enough to give them a friendly word.

I remember a large, pale yellow tomcat who suddenly began loitering around my home one day. He seemed to know when I came home, for he was there every evening. I spoke a few words and meows with him each time. On the third evening he came when I called him, shooting out of the bush and bumping his head so forcefully on my leg that I nearly lost my balance. Then this huge creature threw himself over on his back so I could scratch his belly, as though he were a kitten. He purred like a bubbling coffee pot. Then he sat at my door complaining for an hour to get in. I would have liked to let him in, but I had two rather young kittens, which the street-wise bum would

have certainly bullied. Besides, you can't make a house cat out of an alley cat—well, not easily or very often. He'll still spend hours seeking his freedom, especially when he has a safe haven behind him. An acquaintance of mine had just the opposite experience: A small alley cat that she took into her house was so happy to have a home again that it even kept away from ground floor windows and terrace doors. She was afraid of being put outside in the cold again.

You can always build a loose, occasional friendship with an alley cat if you're not ready yet for the commitment that goes with a permanent house cat in your life. The roaming cat comes by from time to time to enjoy some tidbits, some petting, some dozing on your sundrenched terrace... and then it disappears again. Look out for pseudo-vagabonds. Those are cats that let you feed them, stay several days at your home, and then disappear for awhile. One day you accidentally find out that the large gray cat you called 'Smokey' turns out to be the

beloved 'Peter,' a member of the Miller family a few streets away.

This neighborly cat can generate bitter acquaintances and neighborhood feuds, for not even a license tag is required for cats. A recent article in an American newspaper reported a typical case in which a woman began feeding a kitten that suddenly showed up at her home, where it stayed several hours a day. The lady was hoping the cat would get used to the house and live there. She soon noted that 'Tabby' was getting fatter and fatter. One day 'Tabby' showed up wearing a collar bearing the message: My name is Christine. If you're feeding me, please call this number. The lady called, and the lady at the other end exclaimed, 'Oh yes, about Christine! We've had her three months and you're the fifth caller!'

BUYING A CAT

When you definitely want a cat, buying it is the next step.

There are a number of places from which you can purchase your cat. Many people think of their local pet shop as the first source for buying a cat, and very often they are right. Remember, however, that your pet shop cannot possibly carry every breed of cat. If your pet shop does not have the particular kind of cat that you are looking for, you can check into several other possible sources. One possibility is through the classified pet

These highly held and spirited tail-tips show that these cats (female on left, male on right) are in a good mood and on their way to greet their human companion.

A curly coat characterizes the Cornish Rex. The coat is, unfortunately, very thin, and some naked (that is, hairless) cats are born.

columns of your local daily newspaper. If you find an attractive offer, you've got to decide quickly. Purebred cats are greatly in demand and go fast. That's why you should ask (and listen around) friends, fellow employees and acquaintances...there's always someone who knows someone who has cats of one kind or another.

You could also contact one of the cat clubs and enquire about catteries in your area. The business of catteries is the breeding of show-quality cats, and they sometimes have extra cats for sale. Buying locally is important because you can easily visit the seller if any questions arise about the care of your cat.

It's often worthwhile, if the mother hasn't yet given birth to her litter, to get to know the mother, the father (if he's living in the same household) and, above all, the seller. That will often reveal a great deal about the nature of the breed, which is quite valuable knowledge for the first-time cat owner. A conscientious seller, a true cat lover, will be happy to give you a chance to get to know his cats.

These people often have several kinds of cats, and a prospective buyer of a Siamese, for example, sometimes changes his mind and decides upon a Burmese or Norwegian Forest cat instead. Remember, the seller can be a store of useful information, including the brand of cat food used to wean the kittens; many cats will eat nothing else thereafter.

Where the less seen breeds are concerned, you may have to wait for the kittens to be born. Responsible sellers don't release their kittens before they're twelve weeks old, but it's worthwhile to at least start visiting the kittens from about the sixth week, when they begin to reveal their different personalities. And, of course, you'll want to pick yours out as early as possible.

HARD CHOICES

Now comes the momentous beginning of your life with cats. You have to choose one, and it has to be the right cat for you and vice versa.

My advice is to avoid any advance decisions, not even as to whether you want a tom (male) or a queen (female). Don't make hasty plans to take the strongest kit or the cutest weakling. The last animal born in the litter is always supposed to be the weakest but also the most intelligent and most affectionate. That idea belongs to the old wives' tales about cats, just as do folk sayings about May, June or autumn cats. Every veterinarian will agree that the season when the cat is born doesn't play any decisive role in its chances for a healthy, happy life. So don't bring any prejudices with you when you visit the seller!

Now, the best thing to do is to let yourself be selected. Be patient. All of the cats will show some interest in you after a while. Let them sniff you; hold your hands out to them. Eventually, one of them will come back to you more often, play with you, climb up on you, and make itself comfortable on your lap. (For this activity, I suggest that you wear clothes that will hold up well to being climbed upon, and also protect your skin.)

Pet and scratch the kitten that shows you the greatest interest. Don't pick it up and in no case hold it prisoner. If it voluntarily stays awhile with you, on your lap or leg, plays with your hand and purrs while doing it, then take it: that's the kitten for you. This method of selection doesn't do well only for the kitten: it also favorably disposes your own psyche toward your new feline housemate. During your first weeks together, your little kitten will not only bring you great joy but also all kinds of inconveniences and some loss of your nice disposition. But all displeasure and anger will evaporate once you recall how that little furry bundle adopted you in complete trust when it placed itself in your hands.

BOUGHT AS IS

Playing with and whispering sweet nothings to your new kitten should not completely obliterate your common sense...use your eyes and ears to check out your kitten's health. Are there any exudates or soiled areas? The hindquarters must be clean, without any fecal matter adhering to the anus. Try to recognize the sex while you're at it. An experienced seller would have told you that already, but it's good to be able to do it for yourself.

In male kittens, the anus and genitals are separated further apart than in a female; you can see that only by comparison. In males, the as yet undeveloped genitals look like two dots, while in the female it looks more like an exclamation mark. As mentioned earlier, the sex is really not important in your first cat. It takes on more significance later when you want a second cat.

PEDIGREES AND PRICES

The pedigree of a cat indicates its line of descent: it verifies that the kitten is of the breed stated on it if the pedigree has been certified by one of the cat registries that administrate the world of the cat fancy. You can see ads for cats that state 'no papers,' meaning there's no pedigree with the kitten. Such kittens will, of course,

be less expensive than those whose papers are all in order. If you want a cat only as a companion, then the pedigree is not important; but if you want to show and breed a purebred, then it becomes essential. Otherwise, the cat can be shown only in pet classes. The value of kittens produced will be substantially less than for those who have full documentation. A potential breeder would, therefore, be foolish to buy a cat with no pedigree. The price of a purebred will reflect much about the kitten. One of show quality will be more costly than one which has faults that would prevent it from ever winning. A top breeder will be able to charge more than a person who has no reputation in the breed or

The INNOMED GROOM 'N FLEA PET COMB from Interplex Labs aids in total flea management from head to tail.

is a novice. The rarer breeds may or may not be more costly than the established breeds. You should always take the time to shop around and find out what the normal price is for a pet cat in the breed you like. If you don't do this, you may pay too much money for what might be only a very ordinary cat.

Buying through mail order is, obviously, extremely risky because you do not have the opportunity to see your potential pet firsthand. If you purchase via mail order, it must be from a seller of national repute.

You can sometimes obtain purebred kittens from animal shelters, but the fact that they are there tells you something about the people who put them there in the first place. So, your *best* source for a cat is a local seller who is willing to give you the time and attention that you need to select the right cat for you.

A Persian of the color called "cameo." Persian snouts (or muzzles) have been bred more and more pug-nosed, sometimes causing a breathing problem.

PREVIOUSLY OWNED CATS

Another possibility is to obtain a cat whose owner(s), for one reason or another, is no longer able to keep it.

Maybe they have developed an allergy to cats or they have to move to a house where cats cannot be kept. Sometimes their owner has died; or maybe a marriage has not worked out, and neither partner is able to retain the family pet. These cats are often advertised in local papers, and the fact that the owners have taken the trouble and cost to place the ads does suggest the cat is a treasured pet. Some cats are able to make changes from homes very easily; others are troubled by it and may choose to walk away and try to find their way back to their previous home. They may decide to live on the wild side until they find a home in which they want to live.

CATS FROM ANIMAL SHELTERS

Cats from animal shelters are very needful of extra tender loving care and understanding during the transition. I recently again took a look at cats in a shelter. I am utterly at a loss to understand the cruelty of people in casting away such lovable housemates. Just because of some difficulty, even the problem of caring for a cat during its owner's vacation, hundreds of cats are simply abandoned every year. Many of them land in animal shelters. Because there are so many of these cats, cages are the only way to keep them, and even the most devoted attendants are unable to provide them with even the minimally necessary human attention.

Whether a cat can cope with that for weeks or months, or whether it can ever again form a relationship with human beings, varies from cat to cat. There's unfortunately a great possibility that a cat from such a source will be profoundly disturbed. So a test live-in period can be tried here. However, first find out if the cat hasn't already been loaned out on approval several times before but brought back each time...for if the cat wasn't difficult before, it will most certainly be a problematical cat after such bad experiences. On the other hand, I know of several cases in which cats from an animal shelter have been capable of nothing short of touching gratitude and have become happily attached to their new human companions. They need more attention in the beginning than does, say, a young kitten from a normal environment. These traumatized cats must relearn their natural confidence in humans.

Cats, especially young ones, are often kept two per cage in overcrowded animal shelters. Especially since you're a cat lover, I recommend that you take both of the cage mates home. Two cats that know each other well do better in adapting to a new home than

just one of the two might do. In a later chapter, I'll tell you more about the advantages of having two cats, and there are many of them.

If you're beginning to think that acquiring a cat is rather difficult, I can only agree: yes it is. But the more difficult the beginning of your life together with a cat is, the easier the ensuing lifelong companionship becomes. And that's just the way it should be. The main thing about sharing your life with one or more cats is that you really do want to do this. Give it lots of thought so that you do not become one of those owners who are 'five-minute' cat lovers that quickly tire of their new 'pet' and then ignore or abandon it. These people are the very worst type of owner. But, the fact that you have taken the trouble and expense of purchasing this book suggests that you are not one of them and with good advice will be one of the growing millions of people whose lives are enriched by the company of cats.

The Turkish Angora is a very old breed of cat and was already recognized as such in the sixteenth century. It is slenderer than the Persian and is again coming into fashion in the U.S. and in Europe.

Himalayan. Note the beautiful eyes, which are large and round. The eye color is characteristic of the pointed Himalayan.

Preparing for Your Kitten

Take a long look at your home...it will never be the same again. A cat's home cannot be a doll's house. Let's assume that you don't have any sitting-parlor rooms with Louis XV armchairs or sofas covered with damask or other fine fabrics...which attract cats like magic. Also, the relationship between you and your fully wound-up kitten, especially in the beginning of your life together, could be marred if you happen to have all too many pieces of fine porcelain, glassware, wobbly long-stemmed vases or *objets d'art* around the house. Have no illusions, even with a large home, you really can't barricade or partition off parts of it to keep it catproof...unless you close the doors to those areas and let them undisturbedly accumulate dust. Even then, sooner or later, kitty will slip you and your obstacles and, precisely because that closed-off area will be so pristine and clean, wreck some havoc there. In general, however, your cat will fit in fairly well with any kind of furnishings. Ultramodern furnishings with a great deal of glass, metal and plastic is safe against cat claws, but those furnishings shouldn't be too cold. The cat's natural inclination to coziness must be satisfied with a few accessories: sturdy carpets, pillows or cushions with hard-wearing covers, and niches set off from the main areas of the house. Wooden furniture, whether varnished, polished or natural is generally safe from cat claws. A bit of training, too, can be undertaken. You

Colorpoint, blue: A purposeful cross between Siamese and Persian. Although this breed originated in Europe, it used to be called "Khmer," alluding to the Cambodian people of that name, just to give it an exotic ring.

should also consider some interior rearrangement, maybe remodeling. Even if you're going to let your cat have access to the outside, the young ones have to stay inside at least several months. Later, too, the cat will spend a great deal of its time inside. We still have to discuss the issue of whether your cat will be allowed outside at all or whether it will be completely an inside cat, but this can come later.

BASIC NEEDS

The most important utensils kitty will need are its feeding bowls. You can buy them made of plastic, crock, metal (aluminum or stainless steel, or glass. Functional feeders are flat and don't slide or slip. Even though kitty will eat just as well from an old beaten-up saucer or a discarded salad bowl—as long as it can reach in well enough to get at the food—it's better to use the proper bowls that were designed for cats. You can even buy timer bowls that open and close (like bank vaults) at predetermined times. Such timed feeders can be useful, e.g., to keep the flies off of the food if you're often away for long periods. Or, a timer could be useful if your cat ever needed to diet. Yet others open as the cat stands on a foot plate—again to protect the bowl from flies and to keep the food fresher. But I think these two latter types are really gimmicks that maybe encourage laziness in people. You will need smaller, deeper bowls for drinking. The cat's basic drink is water. You can set a bowl of water right next to the feeding bowl, but you'll find out that a cat doesn't always drink immediately after eating. Some cats tend to use another, more distant source of water, such as a dripping faucet in the bathroom, or a garden pond or simply

puddles of water after rain. I couldn't understand this until experts drew my attention to how large cats in the wild never bag their prey or devour it near watering sites. Quite the contrary: You can observe at African waterholes how predator and prey keep a sort of truce. Eating and drinking are two quite distinct things for a cat. Another bowl for *occasional* milk can go right next to the food bowl; milk is both food and drink for a cat.

It's important to decide where the feeding bowls will be sited, because cats—like most animals, including humans—are very much creatures of habit. It's convenient to select a spot in the kitchen. Most people are drawn there the first thing in the morning and the last thing at night, so the cat's food bowl can be easily checked. Even if your mind is occupied with many concerns, an empty feed bowl has a way of holding your gaze until you think of refilling it.

TIPS FOR INOFFENSIVE CAT TOILETS

Just as important as the arrangements for food and water are those for the cat's fecal matter. A spot has to be found which is always easily accessible to the cat and which is as discreet to the owner as possible. It must be as far from the feeding site as possible. Cats dislike to foul near their food—can you blame them! For some cat

A close relative of the Angora, the Turkish Van is the only cat we know of that likes to go into the water and that swims.

A young kitten carefully takes its first steps into the outside world.

owners, the bathroom is a popular choice as is an accessible patio or maybe a cellar if the cat has free access to this (maybe via a cat-flap door).

The problem of odor should not even arise. An efficient toilet is a central issue in your relationship with your pet. I wouldn't like to live in a home of which my visitors could think (they will rarely say so outright) that it smells badly.Yet this is the truth in some homes and arises because the owners are simply not attendant to the cleaning needs of the cat tray. For this reason, improvisation and trying to save pennies are inappropriate. Obtain a large plastic cat toilet at the very outset. Cardboard or wooden boxes soak up urine and eventually give off unpleasant odors. Two trays are advisable, even for one cat, thus giving you the assurance that your fastidious cat always finds a clean spot to do its duties...instead of who

knows where.

As for the litter that goes into the tray, there are various choices. Some swear by finely shredded newspaper, the shreds of which do make a rather absorbent, odor binding and sterile layer in the box. Others claim that only sawdust does the job right. The most practical (if not the most economical) solution is to buy commercially available cat litter products. These, too, differ in materials used to control odor, provide absorbency, etc. You've got to try it out; a cat will accept several attempts to find the best litter for its toilet box. As with most things you will get what you pay for—the cheap cat litters are far less efficient and odor controlling than the better brands.

THE SCRATCHING POST

A scratching post is really essential for the well being of your kitten, as well as saving your upholstery from being reduced to shreds, which is assured if you do not provide kitty with the means by which it can keep its claws in shape. Remember, a cat has retractable claws, meaning they do not touch the ground like those of a dog, so cannot wear—they must be sharpened on some object. I will interject here that the practice of declawing a cat is both bestial and morally contemptible of an owner—some vets even refuse to attend to this barbaric act. If a person's furniture is so important to his ego that he needs to value it above the well being of his cat, he is certainly no cat lover and would do well to obtain a goldfish.

Scratching posts are readily available from pet shops in various styles and sizes—the biggest are, of course, always the best. Some are fashioned into climbing frames that are both functional and very entertaining. Even if you are a really terrible carpenter, I am sure your talents would extend to nailing some old carpeting around a solid piece of timber. However, commercial scratching posts offer greater variety in terms of design. Whether the cat likes it, you have to try it to find out; whether the cat uses it is a question of training. That is a subject unto itself that will be the source of a later chapter.

THE CAT ARRIVES HOME

Now, your home is, to a certain extent, finally ready for your cat, and you can bring the little guy (or gal) home. Transportation is usually by car. From bitter experience, I strongly urge you to keep the kitten in a container or cat carrier when traveling inside the car. It's best to get a cat carrier at the same time you get the kitten. You'll need it from time to time, such as for visits to the vet, vacations, or maybe to cat shows.

If you try to transport the kitten in your arms, you take the risk of its struggling itself

Four Paws Miracle Malt aids in the prevention and treatment of hair balls. Miracle Malt prevents constipation and helps to eliminate any accumulated hair. Contains vitamins B_1 and E.

free and scampering off down the street, under a car in the worst case. When I picked up my first tom cat Mao as a timid nine-week-old kitty, I turned him loose in my car and had to work half an hour getting him out from under one of the car seats. I had to dismantle the seat! A friend of mine suddenly had his newly collected kitten under the brake pedal, which almost made that the last trip for both the friend and the cat.

This first ride for a kitten is a stressful time. This abrupt change in its life when it is taken from the comforting

SOCIAL DEBUT

You'll eventually reach home and bring an end to the nerve-wracking trip, but do realize that at least the rest of this day still belongs to your kitten. Set the carrier or container in the middle of a room so as to reduce the number of corners your new kitten can crawl off into, then let it come out on its own. Don't pull it out. At this point, the differences in cat characters become obvious, and you can predict future behavior on it. There are kittens that stride out almost at once, and from that

This kitten is very anxious—with its belly pressed to the ground and its tail almost between its hindlegs—as it carefully sets one paw ahead of the other.

warmth of its mother and siblings on a strange and maybe frightening voyage can induce sickness and other conditions. You've got to talk comfortingly and softly to the youngster throughout the trip. The best way to do this is to take a helper along whose main job is to provide the comforting and tranquilizing talk. The driver then concentrates on traffic. This is the beginning of what, with humans, is called bonding, and it commences from the moment you collect the kitten.

moment on begin to inspect everything. They are the enterprising daredevils that you'll have to keep an eye on. There are others that at first don't come out at all and even have a little nap inside the carrying case. Yet others do come out but only to scurry off somewhere out of sight. Your patience is needed now. You don't have to do anything, nor should you. With this type of kitten, all you need to do is to let its curiosity get the better of it, and eventually it will approach you. Then you can

(where it was born) up to now. You can assume that most sellers are well informed and have been feeding their kittens the right diet (in addition to mother's milk). If, on the other hand, your kitten came from a private party (not a breeder) or from a farmyard where it was fed on table scraps, then you've got it easy...it eats what it finds in its bowl. We, of course, put in there only what's good for it, which means a meat-based meal. Let's hope that we don't get a cat from a household where it was pampered with caviar, crab, shrimp and lobster. That happens, too! It's important for the kitten to find its accustomed food, especially during the first few days; later, everything can be changed slowly and carefully. That applies also to feeding times. It's important to realize that a small kitten has a

The Norwegian forest cat is a robust animal. From its coat to its body build, it is adapted to defy the rigors of its northerly home.

interest it in a game by trailing a length of string in front of you. It will soon start to gain in confidence and will then start to explore its new home.

INITIAL FEEDING

The proper feline menu will be discussed in detail later on, so for now we will take things as they come. Once your kitten has arrived in your home it may well appreciate a small meal and a drink of cool fresh water. Give what it has been eating

Reward your cat or kitten with Four Paws Super Catnip products for hours of fun and enjoyment or grow Vita-Greens. Cats love this natural home-grown hairball remedy.

small stomach, but it will grow astonishingly fast during these first few weeks. So it needs many small meals, especially when it's very young, that is, less than twelve weeks old. The recommended feeding is about six meals a day at two-hour intervals. I even recommend, if you work away from your home, taking up to two weeks vacation time to get your new companion started. Then you can carry out this procedure. After that, you can feed your cat just after you get up in the morning, leaving another, small portion when you leave the house. Then, when you come home, give another snack, which holds the cat until its last feeding just before you turn in for the night. If there's any chance of spoilage, say on hot summer days, make the second feeding a dry cat food, which we'll talk about again later. In six months, your kitten will eat enough with only two feedings a day, but with larger portions, of course.

A word about drinking: all of us still hold on to the image of a cat just lapping away at a bowl of milk. That's not a true image. The proper drink for cats, even little ones, is clear fresh water. Milk is more of a food than a beverage, because it contains vitamins and trace elements. Whether, indeed, a cat likes or even tolerates milk is a highly personal matter of taste and experience. Some don't like

milk at all, probably because they never got used to it. The fact is that a cat mother's milk is much richer than cow's milk in fat, and the kitten's digestive system is attuned to the fat content. It would be wrong to give a cat skimmed milk. Diluted condensed milk, with its higher fat content, or even cream, would be better. Many cats get diarrhea from milk, that is, too much of it. Anything more than a scant ½ cup daily will probably be too much. Kittens should not be given milk under any circumstances whatsoever.

USING THE CAT TRAY

If your kitten has come from a good seller, it may already be trained to use a litter tray, so all you need to do is to show it where this is. But even if kitty isn't so trained, it is not a matter of any great concern with cats, which are surely the cleanest of all family pets. After the kitten has eaten, after it has been playing a few minutes, and after it awakes from sleep are the prime times it will want to relieve itself. It will tell you this by turning in little circles and mewing as it seeks a suitable spot. At this moment, you should gently lift it and take it to the litter tray. You must expect the occasional puddle during the first day or so, but very often kittens will take to the litter tray immediately, like a duck to water. If they know where it is, they will use it, providing it is always clean. Praise the kitty every time it

does what is required, and this will reinforce the habit. I have to emphasize once again that absolute cleanliness of the cat's toilet facilities is a precondition to the cat's own cleanliness. Ideally, you should remove fecal matter and urine-soaked litter every time it is deposited in the tray. But you are not always around to do this if you are at work so should make a habit of removing it as soon as you get home. I'm always amused when a guest in my three-cat household sniffs the air and declares: 'But your place doesn't smell of cats!'

What kind of idea does he have about keeping a cat? I, however, am always horrified when I visit a home that indeed reeks of cats. What else are these owners doing wrong?

COMBING AND BRUSHING

From the very beginning, your little kitten, even if it's not long haired, should get used to two things: a comb and brush. Cats have an active molt with seasonal high points. Even the stay-at-home cat has more or less pronounced winter and summer coats; they are

Head study of a Maine Coon. Whether your cat is longhaired or shorthaired, a regular grooming regimen is a must.

is easy because all you need to do is brush lightly, comb and then polish with a nice soft piece of cloth. Longhaired breeds take more time and you should commence by using the brush with the lie of the coat, then against it, then back with it. Next, use a wide-toothed comb

naturally more pronounced in the cat that is allowed outside. Regular grooming, meaning daily, removes dead hairs which otherwise may be swallowed by your cat as it attends to this chore itself, which it will always do—even after you have painstakingly combed it. In addition, grooming the fur gives you a chance to spot any ectoparasites (fleas, ticks) or eczematous areas of skin. With longhaired cats, you can rake out the strangest things that get trapped in the fur and that even the most vigorous licking won't dislodge. Finally, most cats adore this fur care, which helps establish rapport with your cat from the very beginning of your role as its surrogate mother.

Grooming shorthaired cats and finally a narrow toothed. Try never to pull hard, as this will certainly make grooming a displeasurable occasion for the cat.

CATS ARE NOT ANGELS

Now, you've got a little cat at home and, as I mentioned at the beginning of this chapter, your home will never again be a doll's house (if it ever was), that is, a no-touch showroom. No doubt that you're going to find a cat hair or two on the rugs and furniture, perhaps even by the bushel at times. You'll naturally discover a scratch mark on a polished surface from time to time. A cat claw might catch in a curtain, or the drapery, and cause a sort of run in the threads. After all, a little cat is overly active, often crazily playful, but that is what kittens and cats are all about.

Speaking about runs in fabrics, your clothing should be somewhat scratch resistant or, at the least, old so you do not mind a few claw marks or threads during the first few weeks with new kittens. A kitten still has to learn how to manage its sharp claws. You can tell a novice cat owner by the scratches on their hands, just as if they had been picking blackberries! Kittens usually learn quickly that human skin is inferior to feline fur, and from then on really treat you with kid gloves...except when they really have to express themselves about something. Speaking about claws, if you're not inoculated against tetanus yet, then do so. Also, keep a good antibacterial ointment in your medicine cabinet so you can quickly treat minor scratches.

A Maine Coon and a Norwegian Forest. The Forest cat is the larger and more robust of the two breeds.

Cat Training

What a kitten doesn't learn, the cat never will. A cat does what it wants to do. Therefore a cat is unteachable. Many cat lovers are satisfied with this logic and don't even try to train their cats. They get what they deserve. A home in which one or more cats are allowed to do what they want is certainly no well-ordered household, either for the cat lover or for any of his occasional guests. The latter's mounting displeasure will be amply reinforced as Boots and Tabby stride their way over your spread of delicatessen and join guests by helping themselves to a buffet luncheon!

TRAINING OR SPOILING?

The choice doesn't have to be. You can indeed train cats, a fact many owners do not always appreciate. Educating a cat is less vigorous than training a dog; there are more well trained dogs than there are cats because dog owners spend hours, days and even months in training on the exercise grounds, or in the field doing actual work (such as retrieving waterfowl). But cat owners seem unprepared to devote the same efforts into their feline friends. It is as though they are accepting the fact that cats, when compared to dogs, are simply not too bright. The truth is they are every bit as intelligent, but their training needs more thought on behalf of their owners—and this is the limiting factor, not the cat! This said, the cat is not as socially dependent on its fellows as is the dog for its survival. As a result it simply is not as prepared to cooperate as much as a dog, which is essentially a pack animal, just as we humans are. In turn, this means that a cat trainer needs endless patience in order to communicate a nondisciplinary action to a cat.But for day-to-day needs, a cat responds to discipline exactly in the same way as a dog does.

NAMING A CAT

Your kitten begins its training by getting named. Your fantasy can run amok here in this delightful little game with just you and the cat, or socially with family or friends. I suggest that you have your new companion's name all ready for it when it arrives and that everyone involved uses the name. The kitty can't start soon enough learning its name. There's absolutely no doubt that later on you'll come up with some nickname. But referring to the cat's real name is important for communication. Be sure names are easy to pronounce—a few ideas can be gleaned from those chosen by some famous people, who have taken great pains to give just the right names to their cats. Cardinal Richelieu had Felimare, Soumise and a Perruque. Charles Dickens's cat was Williamina. My own cats, past and present, are Mowgli, Einstein, Ophelia, Mao, and Bagheera. The choices of Dennis Kelsey-Wood, the pet-book author, for his eight cats are Clovis, Sulu, Fergie, Domino, Marmaduke, Sophie, Jasper and Rusty. Wittingly or unwittingly, all of these cat namers have done something right: the names contain clear vowels, which behavioral scientists believe make the names easier for the animals to remember. Some people also think that the names should have at least two or more syllables to better distinguish them from simple commands such as No! and Come! So much for that. Have fun in finding or inventing cat names...to which it would really be nice if they always responded! Use the name as often as possible and always so that it ends in a pleasurable act. Since love can be expressed by a nicely prepared meal, the call to dinner is the most important aid in teaching the kitten its name. But always remember a golden rule of animal training: *never* punish a cat for a misdemeanor by calling it to you—its name must always be associated with a pleasurable act.

TABOOS AND NO-NO'S

As with all training, the cat trainer should have a clear idea of just what the purpose

There's nothing with which a cat won't play and hardly anything that doesn't interest it. The saying goes, "Curiosity killed the cat," to which others may add "And satisfaction brought him back."

of the training is. What is expected of the cat? That's a matter of individual preference. The lover of cats will establish a few reasonable taboos for his cats...but only a very few, because more cannot be enforced. I, for example, established two taboos even before I brought my cats home: no cats in my bed and no cats at my table. I've managed a resounding 50% success! Our cats share our bed, at least sometimes, with us. It's very instructive to see why it came to that because it shows how thoroughly the training has to be carried out. When Mao first became a member of the household, the bedroom was closed to him. For five days he cried pitifully just outside the closed door. I turned a deaf ear to him, though it was hard on me, and even harder on the sentimental womanly figure next to me. In two weeks, Mao had apparently gotten used to his cat basket which we set up in a small workroom next to our bedroom. I was triumphant. He had apparently accepted his sleeping spot, just as cat books told us he would.

A month later I decided to leave our bedroom door open like we used to for better air circulation. When I awoke, Mao was sleeping just as comfy as you please at the foot of the bed. And that's where I left him. I had no more appetite for another training cycle!

Some people regard animals in, or on, beds as being unhygienic. Fortunately, however, millions of children sleeping under these life-threatening conditions (of animals in human beds) have grown up to be strong, healthy people! To live with cats means to share your life with them. In general, man and cat can't contaminate each other very much. I see to it that my cats are free of worms and fleas. If I washed my hands every time I petted a cat, like the sanitation fanatics demand, I'd soon be able to pull my skin off like a glove!

There are, however, some limits that must be set. I don't allow cats to stroll around on the dining table, whether we're just about to eat or not. We've enforced that, except for a few relapses. How was it enforced? With persistent watchfulness and thoroughness. From the very beginning, the word *no* was pronounced forcefully and loudly. This was an absolute prohibition for anything that was really undesirable, including shaking the drapes, sharpening claws in the wrong place, and jumping up on the table. As back up to the verbal order, I grabbed the young cat gently but firmly by the scruff of the neck and put it somewhere else. Kittens are used to that because that's how the mother cat tirelessly transports her kittens to just where she wants them. The best remedy is to nip some attempts in the bud; admonitions after the fact have no effect. Only by being caught in the act can the perpetrator make the association with the feeling of discomfort elicited by a loud and stern *no!*

WHEN PUSSYCAT POUTS

Take care that your cat doesn't turn hand-shy from this training. There's a good way to avoid that—the water pistol. You may not think much of it as a child's toy, but it's excellent for training cats. Buy the largest one in the shape of a submachine gun—it has a surprisingly great range. For bad manners, give the cat a short burst, a minimally slight, cold shower, which even the brightest cat won't associate with its human companion. The avenging water strikes, so as to speak, out of thin air. This water pistol is also a very humane way to break up a cat fight in your garden or to discourage a visit by any overwhelmingly belligerent cat from the neighboring turf. Prohibitions and taboos don't so seriously that she immediately rubbed up against our legs until we petted her. She was a sensitive creature who couldn't bear any unhappiness in our relationship.

Training will not eradicate or change some things. You cannot train a cat to pick up morsels from its food bowl and carry them elsewhere to eat them. Also, you can't

Cats transport their kittens over great distances. There are cases in which the mother transported her three kittens one by one, at intervals of fifty yards, for miles.

make you the most popular housemate. Mao and Einstein, for instance, immediately left off whatever bad they were doing when I said *no!*...but they tore through the room, complaining loudly. Einstein especially played the role of what I used to call the wild and murderous cat for five minutes. Don't let all that unnerve you, but watch out that new transgressions are not committed. Ophelia, on the other hand, took rebuke prevent cats from seeking out high resting spots up on the furniture. That's instinctive behavior. Cats that are constantly shoved away from the credenza because your mother's precious porcelain or knick-knacks are kept there will definitely become neurotic. The knick-knacks are in the wrong place.

TRICK TRAINING

Although cats can be trained to do many things, I don't go much for circus-type

Cats are adept and agile and love to climb.

tricks. I really don't want my cats to give a paw on command or stand up on their hind legs and pirouette like a ballerina. They can learn to do it, and I've seen it done. But I don't think it's any fun for them. What cats like to do they often learn alone, which is amazing enough. Every cat can soon learn to use a paw to open a door that's already ajar. All cats grasp the relationship of the doorknob or latch with the opening of the door. When they want to go out, they don't watch the doorpost for the first gleam of light, the obvious place to get out, but they look up at the doorknob or latch that the human companion is operating. In countries with horizontal door handles instead of rounded ones, talented cats learn to jump up and use their weight to depress, and hence open, the door. To be quite frank, I don't wish any

such talented cat on you. Nothing's safe from a cat like that. It's even questionable whether you would want a cat that has learned to use your toilet! I once knew of a Siamese cat that did this. She sat just right on the toilet seat and, after doing her duties, meowed until someone came to flush. Also, I once saw a wondercat use an old-fashioned toilet (with the water tank above and a chain to flush it): on the end of the chain was a tassel...which the cat pulled to do its own flushing!

Cats, then, can be trained to do many things. But for the average cat owner, the thrust of training should be directed at making the cat a respectful member of the family, just as all others are expected to be. Because they are so athletic and have a natural desire to view things from above, rather than from ground level, you will need to be persistent in your desires that they neither jump on the table or kitchen work surfaces nor perch on your curtain rods. But if you expect them never to recline on your bed or on the arms of an upholstered chair, then you are expecting too much. You are advised to seek an alternative pet, because both your life and that of the cat could never be harmoniously in synchronization.

Despite all love, a cat has no business on the table where people are eating. It's best to nip this bad habit in the bud and not to let it even start.

To Be Allowed Out or Not?

Stepping out or not: a question of life and death. I still remember how surprised I was twenty years ago when I began to be interested in *for sale* ads for kittens, to read only for apartment residents. What did that mean? Wasn't a cat a free-ranging predator that lived with man, as Grzimek's animal encyclopedia stated? In my literature on cats I found this statement by a veterinarian: 'Whoever keeps a cat without ever letting it go outside is also capable of keeping goldfish wrapped up in wet handkerchiefs!' That analogy seemed to hold water, at least until I looked into it more closely. The outside world of cats has drastically changed, and for the worst, since that vet made his analogy. It used to be a calculated risk to let your cat out, just as it is today. You take that risk every time you open your door. The decision to let your cat outside is, as dramatic as it sounds, a question of life or death. I'll make your decision easier, though I can't relieve you of it altogether. I'll mention the risks, but you'll have to weigh the pros and cons of your own case. In the first place, there's traffic. Although no statistics are available, experts agree that more cats are run over and killed out in the countryside

and rural areas, in and around villages and small towns, than in large cities. That's mainly because people in those outlying areas are the most likely to think they can let their cats run free. That may be a mistaken notion, depending on the location of your home. The extent of automobile activity can be particularly great there, especially during human sleeping hours when cats are underway. In such rural areas, public traffic devices and safeguards are not as prevalent; also, local by-passes and detours often cut right through ideal cat territories. Drivers really rush through those places. Rural folks seem to have an aversion to seeing anything that creeps or flees across the road, and emergency braking is hardly ever considered for just a stray cat.

In rural areas, cats themselves are less alert to the dangers of traffic. Their main haunts are relatively protected meadows, hedges and forested patches. They have to cross a highway only once or twice while patrolling their territories, when going out and then coming in. Just as for many other animals, the light from auto headlights seems to mesmerize cats. The speed of these four-wheeled killers is too much for even the fastest cats.

In large cities, in contrast, some cats develop into real traffic specialists. Cats that are able to learn from experience, that is, to survive their first freedom outside of their homes, usually confine their travels to areas free of streets. They may regard these areas as natural boundaries. 'May,' I said, because cats too succumb to the idea that the grass is greener, and the mice fatter, on the other side of the street...not to speak of toms and queens being more attractive over there if the cat is still in possession of its reproductive organs! Cats become very careful after successfully surviving a confrontation with an automobile. There was once a huge tomcat in our neighborhood who was thrown by colliding with a car. Luckily, he survived and died of old age when he was eighteen years old. Night after night in our not exactly lifeless neighborhood, he would be on the prowl,

looking for cats. He traveled over busy streets but with excellent pedestrian discipline. He checked both directions for minutes, then finally ran across only when no car was anywhere in sight.

REAL AND PSEUDO HUNTERS

The further you live away from urban areas, the greater loom other dangers. The self-styled hunters in some places consider cats as fair game. They try to justify this

Parked cars unfortunately hold a fatal attraction for cats. They provide a fine hiding spot and also residual warmth from the engine. Many cats don't stand clear soon enough when the driver starts up, leading to injuries and fatalities.

shooting of cats by alleging that they kill birds and small animals such as rabbits. I can only say, to respond to such allegations, that examination of the stomach contents of cats that were shot revealed that the losses in wildlife were minimal, probably mainly sick animals. I recently watched a pet dwarf rabbit effortlessly flee from a moderately sized cat. I can't imagine that a wild rabbit would be any less efficient in escaping, unless it was a baby. In any case, hunters take delight in shooting rabbits and other wildlife just for the fun of it, so who are they to cast stones! Hunters in Germany are legally allowed to shoot cats once they are at least three hundred meters (a little over three hundred yards) beyond built-up areas. That's usually considered very magnanimous...in their own minds. In addition to genuine hunters with licenses, there are also those who buy small-caliber and air guns by mail-order, what I would term pseudo hunters. Modern air guns develop a penetrating force that can seriously wound or even kill cats. My vet friend told me that such wounds are no longer rare in his practice. He's even seen wounds like that in the high-income suburbs of a large city. 'In every area,' the vet said, 'there's an idiot who goes shooting every day. The prey is not only cats but also birds, ducks, dogs and, in extreme cases, children!'

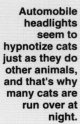

Automobile headlights seem to hypnotize cats just as they do other animals, and that's why many cats are run over at night.

In the country, as well as in the city, there are those animal lovers who are selective about their love. That is, they no doubt ardently love their own dog...who is taught to go get cats. And it's not just the amateurs but the professionals, too, who use cats. A large magazine recently related how hunting dogs are trained to go after and seize prey (simulated by the use of cats!). Now a cat has a good chance against a dog. The cat can shoot up a tree and can use its claws against the first assault. But under the direction of their handlers, many, especially larger, dogs are developed into cat maulers or neck wringers. It's a constant battle with that kind of mentality.

VISIBLE AND INVISIBLE DANGERS

All of the foregoing represents the dangers that cats or you as their protector may encounter. What is really treacherous is the danger of poisoning, which is almost impossible to ward off. In the sections of large cities where there is greenery, such as yards, lawns and landscaping, more and more toxic substances are being applied, both by municipal authorities and by private owners, to a variety of pests and vermin, particularly rats. Most of these substances are

The outdoors poses a number of risks and dangers to the free-roaming cat.

dangerous, or even lethal, for cats. Unfortunately even the most discerning cats often develop an appetite for something like a smelly herring head soaked with rat poison. A poisoned cat is usually diagnosed too late, even by its alert owner. Veterinarians know the story all too well. Certain wood treatment substances and paints for fences and garden sheds, for example, can poison cats. In the mildest case, these substances can cause a temporary loss of fur.

That's a worrisome array of risks. So, do we let the cat out or not? Whoever has seen cats radiating joy, going wild, or just stalking a flower in high grass, climbing branched trees, and running across fields, will let their cat out whenever possible. That can be done under certain conditions, but only with the greatest precautions, and after responsible evaluation of any risks.

You may live in the country or in a tight little community somewhere where everyone knows everyone else's wife, husband, children, relatives and livestock...and feels responsible for them. The hunter who leases hunting rights near your property takes care not to shoot at your cat because he remembers how good your cognac was, or other little niceties you offered him at one time or another. Your neighbor lets you know he's putting out pesticides or painting his fence. The neighbor's kids retrieve strayed cats, or even those that haven't quite strayed yet, for a tip. You'll receive neighborly reports on the comings and goings of your

Facing page:
**The inside cat
needs at least
an opening—
window or
balcony—to the
outside world.**

cats, and with that information you can sometimes take some precautions.

Another danger to outside cats, especially if they are kittens, is predators, depending if they are native to your locality. For example, coyotes, especially in the country areas of the north and western regions of the USA, take a heavy toll of kittens. Sulu, the Siamese belonging to cat author Dennis Kelsey-Wood, was bitten by a rattlesnake in the pasture of his New Mexico home (miraculously, it survived the two bites). The fox is yet another ever present threat to young cats, as are eagles, buzzards, and other birds of prey in country areas.

I should also mention the human predators, those utterly contemptible people who, too lazy to earn an honest living by working, choose to steal pedigree dogs and cats, as well as exotic birds, and sell these to whoever will buy them— including research establishments.

You can of course provide your cats with an outside fenced enclosure, a sort of large aviary, and many breeders do this. Personally, however, I find that is too much like a kennel or a zoo for my taste. Anything short of a totally enclosed area would be ineffective in restricting a cat so, other than a zoo-like enclosure, the choice is either taking the chances and letting the cat be

free roaming, or keeping it indoors. Let's understand that a cat with stepping-out privileges is a worrisome affair. There'll be sleepless nights when you'll give a start every two hours because you thought you heard a familiar meow by the window or door. You'll have to bother your neighbors with questions, like whether they've perhaps inadvertently locked your beloved cat in their tool shed or cellar. That happens more often than you realize. Cats look for and investigate such places out of curiosity but fade out of sight at the approach of any strangers. At one time or another, you may be the helpless witness of heroic cat fights and then have to minister to the wounds of one of the warriors. That will no doubt be the loser, often your little darling, that is not quite as street wise as the local tom, who is king of the neighborhood, attested by its chewed ears and battle-scarred face! All of these events naturally enrich the cat lover's repertoire of anecdotes...which are recounted only after everything is over and has turned out for the best. Think carefully about the illusions of nature or naturalness. If you want to offer your cat as natural a life as possible, then you will expose it to all of the dangers of nature and life in the wild, as well as to the dangers of our civilization...and these may mean injury or even death.

THE HOUSEBOUND CAT

For all of these reasons, the cat that lives exclusively inside the home is no longer a rarity. Indeed it is becoming quite the norm, especially where valuable purebreds are concerned and which are living in cities. When the situation warrants, the true cat lover need have no second thoughts. Since cats cannot decide an issue rationally, we have to do it for them. Some cats do, however, decide to lead a more confined existence as a result of some traumatic happening. One outside-inside cat was run over by a car and didn't want to go outside anymore once its wounds healed. Another cat finally had enough of the neighborhood's many dogs, so preferred to hiss and spit at them from a high-placed first floor window rather than within biting distance. A small tomcat, who had just recovered from his premier bout with a stray cat twice his size, decided based upon this principle: my home is my castle. A cat poll would show an ever-increasing preference for the comfy seclusion and safety of the human companion's home, not the wild outside world.

THE INNER SANCTUARY

A human home must offer the cat some of the things the cat would find out in the wild. That is, the home, at least parts of it, must represent a feline's landscape, a cat's playground for its modest adventures about the home and grounds. That implies at least a minimally adequate area. At least two separate rooms, according to experts. A cat must be able to retire...disappear from view. An older, perhaps rambling house is ideal. It's usually roomier than a recently constructed one. It has more corners and niches (the favorite haunt of a cat is a sort of den, high perches or observation platforms). Also, an older house is not decorated as functionally modern as new constructions, thus leaving a variety of cat-friendly hideaways and play areas.

I know a lady who has set aside one room of her old, five-room house as a rumpus room for cats. Gaily painted tree trunks with many branches go from floor to ceiling and wall to wall, giving her four cats a marvelous playground on which to discover the utmost in feline felicity. Each cat has its own personal spot in the branches where it can rest and ward off any unwanted dance invitations or challenges.

All of that expense and remodeling is naturally not necessary, only a little imagination is needed. In contrast to that splendid cat room, I have a friend who lives with an elegant brown Havana cat in a large, one-room apartment. Havana cats are vivacious and fastidious. That small apartment consists of a large room, kitchen niche, bath and balcony. A whole corner of the living room is dedicated to a sitting landscape. White

undecorated book cases line the walls. And what about the cat? Don't worry, that's all taken care of with a hidden subterranean complex!

THE HIDDEN SUBTERRANEAN COMPLEX

Under the sitting landscape in the mentioned one-room home lies a clever subterranean complex of tubes, conduits, and passages of cardboard and styrofoam. They open into others built into the closed bases of the bookcases. Unbelievable stalking trails abound. Openings are everywhere so the cat can take an occasional peek at what you and your visitors are up to, or so somebody can toss a ball down into one of the tubes. The passages lead under the heating

An almost ideal cat tree—solid wood with sisal fiber for scratching—that provides resting platforms at various heights, a hole to hide in, and little balls on rubber cords for play.

system and as far as the balcony door, in which a spring-door can be opened to the outside. Half of the balcony, the summer half, is enclosed with fine mesh netting.

The cat can sit there, sun itself, clean itself, and look at the birds and all else that is on view. On the balcony there's also a large plastic tub planted with fresh grass, the tips of which a cat likes to nibble from time to time. 'If this human being, with whom I share my home,' the cat may well think, 'has that intolerable jerk over again to visit, the one who always wants to handle me, then I can retreat to my private complex. The small bulb in there keeps me wonderfully warm, and I've got a perfect right to claw any human hand that pokes around in the box. After all, a cat's got to have some privacy.'

So, with a little imagination and sensitivity, you can make a cat sufficiently comfortable and also keep it active, even in a small apartment. In addition, commercially made cat trees are useful, especially if you integrate them into your decoration. Balconies, terraces, and roof gardens are a blessing to cats. Many people, however, think that cats are, by nature, free of dizziness in high places and can climb around and even jump quite safely on window sills, balcony ledges, and roofs. That is often a mistake, a fatal one.

Cats are indeed very skilled climbers, but you can't assume that they never take a false step. Any cat you hear about that survived a fall from the fifth floor all the way down to a paved street is an extremely lucky cat indeed. Most would either be killed or very badly injured. Cats often react instinctively, say to unexpected noises or passing birds, and that can suddenly cancel out their famous powers of equilibrium. The cat lover should place easy-grip covering on window ledges on the higher floors, with screening if these windows have to be opened. Balconies, too, need a catching device. The best designs are the anti-suicide screens on high observation terraces and on bridges. I know what I'm talking about: Ophelia came bounding out from somewhere inside my home and with a single leap hit the balcony railing...and hung on to it by only two paws, with nothing below her but over fifteen feet of air. By the time I reached her, she had already managed to pull herself up on the wooden balcony railing. Had it been concrete instead of wood, I doubt she would have saved herself. I know a man who lost two fine Siamese cats because he let them play on the roof terrace on the seventh floor of his home. One day they played too roughly and were later found all tangled up together in a heap, dead, down on the street.

THE LEASH

A cat can also get around outside like a dog does, on a

leash. For a dog, that's more or less natural, since in a pack of his wolf ancestors (or indeed even his wild wolf cousins today), he would simply follow along in the invisible traces of the whole pack behind its leader. For a cat, however, the leash is rather unnatural. Some people recommend getting your cat used to a leash for visits to the vet, travel or moving. Personally, I prefer using a cat basket or carrying case, which at least provides the cat with the secure feeling of hiding out in a small den. I've tried several times to get cats used to a leash. We really suffered, the cats and I, and at one point or another I gave up. I'm probably too impatient a person, or else I had impatient cats.

The thought finally occurred to me that I really didn't know just what I'm

supposed to do with my cat on a leash. Take a walk? The word *walk* doesn't even come near describing how a cat moves. A cat pussyfoots, pads, saunters, meanders along through its territory. Any halfway normal human being would find it frustrating to try to keep pace. If a real or imagined enemy pops up, where would the cat go? It would most certainly make a beeline for the leash holder and use him or her as a tree for refuge. What happens when it's some huge dog that spooks your cat?

Another problem is using a leash in the garden or, say, at a picnic in the park. Cats tend to struggle and strangle themselves when any interesting prey pops up, and it doesn't make much difference whether they're wearing a collar or an otherwise quite practical

This young lady is doing something foolhardy with her cat. If something should suddenly startle the cat, it could bolt and perhaps tumble off of the roof. Even cats don't always survive such falls.

harness. The great advantage of the latter—if it is a well-made and correctly fitting *cat* harness—is that you can more easily gather the cat in your arms if you see a dog or anything that might frighten your feline. However, all realities considered, I don't think it is a good idea to try and make a dog out of your cat. If you have a need to take a pet for a walk it would seem that a small canine would fit the need far more adequately than a cat.

THE OUTING CAT

A few cat owners have told me that they can take a walk with their cats on weekends in remote areas. They release the cats and assure me that they don't roam further than about twenty yards away. That sounds reasonable since a cat would stay near its human buddy in unfamiliar surroundings. But the human buddy would have to possess superhuman patience. He would have to stop and wait, of course, until the cat sniffed, stalked and lay in wait for one thing or another. Such expeditions are even reported to yield a nice bag of mice and beetles. After a certain time, one or two hours, say my informants, your inside-outside cat gets bored and comes back to you. It's no problem then putting the cat back into its carrying case and driving off with it.

The danger with such outings is that despite careful selection of the grounds, strangers (both human and canine) can pop up and spook your unsuspecting cat. Retrieving a cat from a forest tree is obviously much more difficult than getting it down from a tree in your own garden. Also, the cat may choose to run and hide some distance from you. Dennis Kelsey-Wood and his wife Eve have traveled and lived in England, Spain and the USA, always taking the family cats with them. Apart from the fact that they lived in 11 homes in 14 years, and traveled extensively across the USA in a motorhome, only one cat was ever permanently lost—and the cats were always allowed out of the motorhome at every stop! Dennis says that 'you must really know the personality of each cat, they must want to stay with you, and traveling stops must be picked with care.' Cats obviously do learn how to survive with constantly traveling owners! Some urban cat owners who have a country weekend retreat, often with some land around it, let their cats roam freely on weekends. Here, too, are good and bad experiences. Some people report that their cats know exactly when you're taking them on a weekend trip and jump right into their otherwise disliked cat carriers. The only problem these people have is convincing their cats to go back home with them. The cats learn quickly that on Sunday afternoon their freedom is at an end. So, at that time they tend to disappear, often leaving their owners to go home without their cats...and come back Monday after work to find them. By that time the cat has had enough of its boring and often dangerous freedom...it is hungry and comes willingly if it has survived its night in the wild unscathed. That's a game of nerves. Many cat owners have such, but I don't.

A Zurich cat research specialist whom I highly regard, Dennis C. Turner, lets his own cats run free and accepts the risk that their life expectancy may be less than that of purely inside cats. Although we occasionally lose a cat, which obviously is painful for me, at least I know for a fact that they fulfilled their feline needs, joined in our lives when they wanted to, and, all in all, enjoyed nature with all of its good and bad aspects. Turner naturally deals professionally with a multitude of cats, so replacing a loss is no problem for him. I call this method of keeping cats, which I too am unfortunately forced to use, the calculated concern method. I say *forced* because years ago we moved into a home that seemed to provide an ideal cat preserve. The yards and gardens of the neighborhood form a sort of park, are completely separated from the street by houses and walls for long stretches, and are bordered on the other side by a watercourse. That all creates a sort of natural preserve. We let the two cats we had at that time run free through that area, and nothing ever happened to them. All of their five successors have already fallen into the water two or three times, and at least five times for our clumsy Mowgli. We lost two cats presumably because they tumbled into the freezing water and suffered a heart attack from the cold shock. After these fateful blows, we tended to keep the survivors or newcomers as purely home cats.

Yes, we *tended* to keep the cats home, but that's not feasible with cats who have already tasted the outside life or who see their peers who are indeed enjoying it (we have a cat-operated spring door). Such cats are impossible to keep (happily) locked up inside. They'll unnerve you with their wailing. They'll commit (or perform) really desperate acts to get out. If you do succeed in keeping them inside, they'll just sit and worry as though in a depression. Such a cat is more at risk locked in than it would be traipsing around outside. I did warn you: it's nerve wracking and heart rending. If you want to protect both nerves and heart, bring your cat up as a homebody. Turner says, 'It's certainly not inhumane or cruelty to animals to offer a cat a world of experience inside of the home. The precondition, however, is to obtain a cat that knows only home life, or is young enough to adapt to it.'

Keeping Two or More Cats

The cat is a loner and a jealous protector of its territory, so is best left alone. This is one of the numerous misconceptions that many people uncritically accept. Such a pronouncement robs them and their cats of a whole chunk of good living. For years I've been arguing that it's easier and more pleasant to live with two cats rather than merely one. I doubt that there is a cat expert in the world who would disagree with this viewpoint. You don't have to spend any more time or effort, and you get twice the fun. You can also rest easy in your mind with the knowledge that your cats will definitely be happier during all those times you are away from home. The myth of the loner is exploded just by the fact that a cat gladly takes up life with a fellow or supercat in the form of a human being. This human being, however, if he or she is normal, is overburdened as the only buddy and life interest of his or her cat. The cat, too, is at least as egoistical as a child and wouldn't object in the least if its fellow cat, that is, you, made it the central interest in your life. That does indeed happen to some extent, though I find such a situation unnatural.

What's natural is for the cat owner, especially a working one, to have a few other interests besides his cat. Even the most ardent of cat lovers doesn't rush home every evening to play with his cat, or neglect his social contacts, or give up an evening out with friends and fellow employees. Even the cutest of pussycats won't substitute for a movie, theater or concert evening.

That increases the cat's time alone every day to ten to fourteen hours. True, much of that time is dozed or slept away, but when you come home at after midnight, not much petting and playing is left in either you or the cat. Then you've got the weekends, which the stressed working man or woman needs to recuperate and not to play exclusively with the house cat. In short, the cat is alone quite a lot, and that certainly doesn't please it. When we had our first cat Mao, we were somewhat younger and more active. When he was about nine months old, we left him alone for the weekend for the first time. He cried so pitifully that our friendly neighbor—who was only supposed to fill the food bowl—stayed with him. When we returned, Mao was in real disarray, and it took a

whole evening of intensive rough housing together before we more or less reestablished normal relations. From that time on, Mao always reacted as if he were markedly allergic to the appearance of suitcases and traveling bags. He usually sat on or in them in order to prevent their being filled. All of our subsequent cats picked up this habit, so now we always pack secretly!

REASONS FOR A SECOND CAT

At that time, with Mao, I had the idea that two cats might be better than only one. And, as so often happens when you take on a new interest, I suddenly met

cat lovers with exactly my own sentiments; they owned two or even more cats, and their experiences were very good with them. In contrast, there was the lady who kept forty cats in a shed, a terrible example of the stark difference between a community-like household and a ghetto of them. Keeping a mass, a crowd, of cats is more akin to cruelty to animals. Keeping only one cat can also be cruel.

How do you get two cats? The simplest way is to adopt two from the same litter. There's no problem of adaptation: both kittens make a smooth transition from their natural cat family to your human one. The first-

Cats don't get bored around other cats. Whoever is away from home a lot should give his cat a playmate.

time cat owners may, of course, not always be prepared for life with two cats yet. They'll first want to see how well they do with one. Later, there'll be a time when a newcomer will have to be brought into the household. That generally goes well if the newcomer is still young and also smaller than the incumbent house cat. The older cat knows it's the dominant one, and the younger one accepts lower status because that's how life in the litter was. My optimism in these matters probably stems from our initial success. When I brought Ophelia home to Mao, I let her out of the box and, her tail straight in the air, she ran into the living room, where Mao was resting. He took one look at the new cat and struck a classic pose directly out of a textbook on animal behavior: a firmly planted stance, hair on end and a warning hiss. Then the kitten's tail thickened as she hissed and retreated to a corner. Mao retired into a low bookshelf. Ophelia ventured forth from her corner in order to examine everything in great detail. She immediately tried out the cat toilet and ate the reserve morsels in Mao's food bowl.

Meanwhile, Mao carefully approached for another hissing and spitting exchange. We didn't interfere but stayed ready in case of any serious developments. About half an hour later while they were prowling restlessly around the room, we suddenly noticed that Ophelia, the kitten, was challenging Mao, the tom, to play tag (or cat and mouse?). She jumped a few times right in front of him, then remained still a moment to challenge him. In an instant the ice was broken and both of them whooshed through the whole place until the pursued cat was cornered, at which point the pursued turned and sounded a warning to the pursuer, who then took off again but this time as the pursued cat. They seemed tireless. We went on with our normal domestic activities and may have missed some intermediate phase if there indeed was any. The next time we looked at these two, they lay together on Mao's favorite fur blanket. That's the way they usually slept from then on.

This household cat team consisted of a young female and an older, neutered male. People often ask what the best combination of sexes is. According to my own experience and research, a male and a female almost always go well together, regardless of which sex is the oldest. A tom is always tolerant of the female. An older female, who can be very vicious in territorial matters, has a tendency to adopt small kittens and pour out her frustrated motherly instincts, all of which can develop into full-blown tyranny if we don't step in to moderate the situation.

Likewise, an older male generally accepts a kitten,

but after some ritualized threat posturing. That, however, doesn't exclude some future test of power and dominance once the kitten has grown up. Then, a few pieces of fur may fly amid the battle cries of the combatants. I don't know of any serious injuries from this kind of hierarchical shuffling. We act only as observers, unless dire circumstances call for our arbitration. In general, the males eventually become friends, a friendship that can also include the neighbors' cats. Without reinforcing any more prejudices, I must frankly report that problems are most likely to erupt between two female cats. That is, without a doubt, due to their biology. Every female mother-to-be instinctively attempts to ensure a good start for her upcoming litter of offspring. This includes a territory that is as large and undisturbed as possible. Every other female cat in her territory reduces her mating possibilities as well as the supply of food, hence is a competitor. Usually, however, two female cats eventually get along, and, when the relationship is really good, can even nurse one another's litters.

I'm often asked if two grown cats can be kept together. Today, especially, cat-induced allergies (some of which can be life threatening)

Two cats can be of one heart and one soul, helping one another in coat care, and even against enemies. There are usually no difficulties in getting them used to one another.

CAT SCRATCH from Designer Products, Inc. The large scratching area allows kitty to hone his claws to his heart's content.

are suddenly popping up, making the unhappy victims of the allergy wring their hands in desperation as they search for good homes for their cats, hopefully in homes already blessed with cats. It is indeed possible that fully grown cats can become friendly towards one another, and I know of some. But it takes time, effort, real concern, as well as nerve-wracking and anxious moments...and even then it doesn't always work out.

INCOMPATIBILITY

There are cats that meet and can't stand one another from the very first moment. There is no apparent reason, and that escapes the cause-and-effect mentality of human beings. It has to do with each animal's personal space. If their mutual distaste becomes physical and breaks out in fights which, with cats, are always meant to do bodily harm, then you've got to send the newcomer away. The incumbent cat of the house always has priority, even if the newcomer is ever so cute. It's important to arrange for this give-back possibility beforehand, even if you're bringing a young cat home to an older one. In this case, too, there often appears to be insurmountable aversion, but you can wait somewhat longer than with an adult cat to see if it works out.

In general, however, two adult cats will come to get along well in a household. They may even sleep together and eat out of the same bowl. The degree of friendship may well be governed by the number of other cats in the household. The more there are, the greater the possibility that any extra adults will be tolerated rather than becoming big buddies with the others, though friendships may well occur. At feeding times each cat in the family should have its own bowl and each bowl should have exactly the same food. Each of the cats, however, thinks that the other cat's bowl contains all of the delicacies of cat heaven, while its own contains the worst possible garbage. So they try to eat from each other's bowl. Hierarchy will come into play here, though not always. A greedy individual will glutton from its fellow's bowl and then return to eat its own. You must watch over your cats at feeding time because the more timid ones may get pushed out altogether. In any case you can then notice if any are showing no interest in their dinner, which might be the first outward sign of an impending illness.

Cats can become good friends and buddies. When they meet even after a short separation, they renew their friendship by bumping noses and rubbing heads.

CAT CAMARADERIE

Contrary to popular opinion, a sort of mutual aid society, an *esprit de corps*, develops between (or among) cats that live in the same household. When we still had Mao and Ophelia, the neighbor's overstuffed black-and-white cat Mimi often came to visit me at my desk. Mao ignored her royally, while Ophelia hated her with fiery passion. Mimi was afraid of our little black she-devil and usually fled.

One day, however, she had a run-in: After I had given her a few doses of scratching and petting, she was ready to leave. Just at that moment Ophelia appeared and stood in the way, blocking Mimi's departure. Without much ado, Ophelia pounced upon Mimi. As fur began flying and the screeching reached fever pitch, Mao charged into the fray and bit unhesitatingly right into poor Mimi. I arrived at the scene only in time to help her escape. Mimi would have never fought with Mao had Ophelia not been involved. But cats are not like dogs, who can always be counted on to help out their buddies. They seem to wait awhile to see if indeed their help is needed. But they also assess how powerful the antagonist is. After all, there is little point in aiding a friend if you end up taking a bashing yourself and if it does not affect in the slightest the end result! Even within the same cat family you will be able to discern camaraderie if you keep a few cats. One may help out the other if it is being bullied.

THREE IS THE CRITICAL NUMBER

So there you have some insight into life with two cats. But suppose, for one reason or another, you want more, say just three, cats? Well, that's more difficult. The arithmetic doesn't always click. Two cats often form a clique, which excludes any third cat as an outsider, who then has a tough life.

I once knew a lady who lived in peace and harmony with her friendly house cat Muhle. One day she decided to breed Abyssinian cats, so she brought one home. Muhle, the incumbent cat, got along quite well with her. When this new cat threw her first litter, the lady kept one daughter for breeding. Mother and daughter got along just fine...suddenly leaving Muhle as the outsider. Both of these purebred females kept Muhle, who was very interested in the new litters, away from them. The two mothers chased her from her food, even from the cat toilet. They treated her so badly that poor Muhle retreated to an old sofa in a small room because she had lost any confidence in herself to go anywhere else in the house. Muhle was already somewhat older, and now she suffered from one illness after another, went blind and finally died. That's a sad but true story.

Events are not always so

dramatic, but you've got to consider all ramifications whenever you want more than two cats. If you should keep larger numbers of cats, even if their number is divisible by two, one of them often becomes the black sheep of the group. This depends upon the size of their territory. If there is ample space, the outsider or the black sheep can withdraw to a life of its own, which will be mainly with human beings. This cat's jealous fellows can still manage to disrupt the outsider's relations with its human companions.

These jealous fellow cats, as a matter of fact, are even jealous of each other. If we pet and scratch one of them, it's a sure bet that another one will come up and interfere until the one being petted gets nervous and leaves. This interfering cat, however, may not even want to be petted and is quite satisfied to have messed up the other's petting session. In summary, the joy of living with one cat is at least doubled, if not tripled, when you expand to two cats. The joy can also be merely in realizing that you are doing a good turn for both cats. The good is obvious. Two cats together remain young in heart and playful longer. They tolerate separations and absences from their human companions much better. There are fewer problems

Scientists believe that cats are the only other species besides the higher primates (man, monkeys and apes) that can learn by observation. Unfortunately, as this picture shows, they also learn undesirable daredevil tricks from other cats.

with lack of appetite and finicky tastes, which occur more often when a cat is the only one of its kind in a family. Healthy competition at the food bowl keeps two or more cats well. Please realize that the keeping of several cats instead of only one or two, of course, does not mean less wear and tear on your home and its furnishings. At our home, the cats have a raging session at least once a day. Then the wild chase begins across tables and chairs. Pursuers and pursued alternate. It's apparently considered to be a stroke of tactical cat genius when one speeding cat suddenly leaps to a higher level, takes the high ground, and leaves the other dolts down there dashing about in empty space. If that high ground happens to be the back of a leather easy chair, and a few claw marks eventually show up on it...so what?

I will end this chapter by quoting Kelsey-Wood on just some of the joys of living with eight cats. 'The first thing you learn is that you can indeed sleep on just four inches of king-sized bed without disturbing the felines sprawled over the rest of it as you turn in your sleep. You also become adept at coping with cramp because you do not have the heart to kick the cats off your legs, on which they are snugly curled up. You will become expert in the duties of doorman. As assuredly as one cat is complaining to go out, another will be wanting to come in moments later. If you are not opening doors, you will be opening cans of meat. Your felines take little notice of the bulletin board which clearly states when their feeding times are. There is always some pitiful howling to let you know this or that cat did not gets its meal at the last sitting. If you ignore their pleas, they will simply start to climb all over you until you do get up from your chair or leave off whatever you are doing. Still, think of the benefits of this. You never become addicted to TV because you never see the start or end of anything! When eventually you determine to haul your tired frame to bed, you fumble 'round in the darkness because your darling wife, who is the main reason these felines are there in the first place, has retired earlier, so you do not want to put the light on. As you pass by the bed covers, a paw suddenly flashes out from beneath these to waken the nerves in your feet. You hop around on one foot while mumbling that you will render fatal injury to that kitten beneath the bed, then you bang the toe of your surviving foot on the bed post. By this time you have stumbled around to your side of the bed only to see the figure of your spouse sprawled over it because she has steadily been moved across the bed by the procession of cats that, having had no more than twelve hours sleep during the day are, quite naturally, dead on their feet. The poor little things!'

Neutering And Spaying

It's really not surprising why cats have been either adored or persecuted as a sex symbol throughout the ages. There is hardly any animal that declares (really, advertises) its love so unabashedly and vociferously. Even confirmed

that softens stone...and that can turn human beings raging mad. Both cat sexes participate in this love concert, though the male has the leading role.

Technically, the tom is said to be in rut, and the queen 'calling' or in heat (estrus) or

Once a female cat in heat shows up, it's goodbye to friendship among mature tomcats. They lay back their ears and intone their battle cry. In this scene, the next action will be at least an exchange of paw blows.

cat lovers reach for hard objects or else fill up buckets with water when cats sing and speak of sex under a full moon...and under the cat lovers' bedroom windows!

This cat wailing sounds like a dozen abandoned babies who are hungry, wet, frightened and sick. Victor von Scheffel, a German writer, described it as a noise

in season when they ready to attend matters relating to the continuation of the species. The male is capable of amorous activities all year around and really jumps to the siren songs of calling females. He reacts to the pheromones (hormonal-produced attractable scents) that direct him to the females. In the spring, all tomcats are enterprising and make longer patrols than usual. Male cats in a neighborhood who otherwise get along with one another get involved in preemptory strikes (that is, preventive fights), even in the absence of any females in heat in the vicinity.

TOM CATS

A male cat grows up to maturity in about a year, and that's when the problems start. In my opinion, a sexually mature and whole (still in possession of his testicles) tom absolutely cannot be kept without outside privileges, and then only under certain conditions. A tom will leave his calling card as a lover. He sprays it. The description of that scent is very understated, even if we called it a lion and tiger house smell (like at the zoo).

A tomcat who is allowed outside will cover his whole outside territory with the scent, which appears to support the hope that he'll use up all of his spray supply before he comes back inside. No such luck. Our logic is not cat logic. He'll often also immortalize his favorite spots inside the house with his permanent perfume. Ordinary commercially available deodorants, spot removers, detergents or other cleaning substances won't remove the odor. If you do manage to find a remedy, it might be vinegar water. In your own interest, and that of the people who share your home (or even just

visit it), the situation should not be permitted to deteriorate to that point.

Breeders usually keep their stud cats in tiled rooms isolated from their living quarters, or in outdoor catteries. I've been in homes where tomcat studs were kept without such restraints. The owners usually avowed to have used clever methods to prevent their cats from spraying scent. My own nose, however, told me better. No one can hold it against a tom cat whose only territory is inside the house if he, as he perceives it, sprays a maximal perimeter defense around the whole place.

Another danger that shouldn't be underestimated is that a frustrated tomcat will do everything but everything to reach the object of his affection. Suicide attempts by these cat Casanovas to break out into love's paradise outside have been reported. A tom I know of jumped right through a closed window. He survived after some heavy repairs and was finally 'defused' by being neutered.

A love-mad cat is also a demonic fighter. Kittens that have just become sexually mature get into risky scuffles with older cats, which inevitably gives the youngsters the shorter end of the stick...often also with shorter (that is, torn off) ears and tails!

Animal behavior investigators, especially Paul Leyhausen, discovered some time ago that cat fights are not only ritualized or subject to any rules but also are meant to do bodily damage. The object is to disable the opponent both as a fighter and as a reproducer. The underdog (or should it be the undercat!) can't act in any ritualized way to appease the victor (like dogs do when they strike the humble pose of rolling over and exposing a bare belly, implying 'You wouldn't really bite me in my unprotected belly, would you?'

Leyhausen, however, thought that cats don't receive serious injuries because the victorious attacker indeed does respond to the defensive motions of the loser and doesn't want to risk any prolonged fight to the finish. He also thought that the loser could usually escape without being pursued. Well, apparently all cats have not read Leyhausen's books, for I've personally saved a seriously injured young male cat from two rivals who followed him almost into the house.

And as to the seriousness of the wounds, veterinary bills record the sad story. An unaltered (non-castrated) tom doesn't get any handsomer over the course of years but carries an array of memorabilia like chewed-up ears, impressive facial scars, hairless patches of skin, and often even deformed paws.

QUEENS

Females are generally sexually mature at about 9 months of age. Purebred cats, especially Siamese, often mature earlier and show signs of love's madness as early as 5-6 months. A cat that is 'calling' in the house is a real headache. She prowls restlessly around, cooing continually from deep down in her chest. If you haven't heard sounds like that yet, then you don't know what voluptuous means. Every once in a while, at shorter and shorter intervals, the

The beginning of a squabble: Venomous (sounding) hissing and screaming, and one paw ready to strike. In a moment the left cat will jump the other one.

cooing raises in pitch to loud, that is real loud, screaming. In between these vocalizations, the cat throws herself down, rolls ecstatically around, and frantically licks her teats and genitals. She often presents herself for mating by leaning on her front elbows, raising her hindquarters and holding her tail at high mast, or else bending the tail to one side.

When Ophelia went into her first heat, I was apparently her choice of partner. Her buddy Mao, who had already been put out of commission as far as his love making was concerned, didn't even give her a second glance. She followed my every step. I constantly had a cat under and between my feet who didn't let up rubbing herself against my legs, and wail, wail, wail. You can take all that humorously and make family-rated jokes about it, but the fact is that the female was suffering— and I along with her.

A female cat goes through a natural cycle that puts her in heat two or three times a year. Artificial lighting and other factors involved in living with human beings, however, can lead to cats being in heat every two months, even every month. The literature describes nymphomaniac Siamese queens who are continually in heat. That's a real torment for those animals. They hardly eat and lose weight. Their glossy coats turn dull and unkempt, and they tend to get skin conditions and shed much more hair than usual. So, in every respect, it's also a mess for their human companions.

BIRTH CONTROL IS A MUST

Some people take all that as part of the bargain because they eventually want their cats to have kittens. Many of these people want to do that for their cats' happiness, and others want to do it only for themselves. Responsible cat lovers, however, must forego this pleasure. There are enough homeless cats already. Visit any animal shelter...no, on second thought, don't if cat misery goes right to your heart. There is simply no reason for a cat to produce kittens unless for a specific reason, such as when breeding for show quality or new colors. Left to themselves, females will produce large numbers; to quote the well-known phrase 'they can breed like rabbits.' A normal litter consists of 3-4 kittens, though a cat can give birth to 6 or more and still provide them with milk. Two or three litters a year are possible.

The uncontrolled production of cats leads to those sad populations of cats in the streets of Rome, Paris, New York and elsewhere, even Germany, where a plague of cats was reported. These cats eventually land in a shelter, which is already bursting at the seams. Most will end up with lethal injections or being sold to experimental laboratories, so think on this when you fail to have your cat desexed.

SPAYING AND NEUTERING

The true cat lover has, therefore, more than enough good reason to prevent unwanted reproduction before it is even possible. It is effected by castration for males (neutering) and removal of the uterus (spaying) for females.

Many people react in a very human way: The poor cat. He won't have any more fun now! These people don't realize that sex is only a drive in animals, a mechanical or automatic push. A drive like that can seriously endanger a cat, make it aggressive, cause it to suffer, and even make it sick. Besides, even if the cat were being deprived of an experience, it wouldn't realize it. What you haven't had you can't miss! Up to recently, the timing of the castration operation was a debated issue. Operating too early, say at 5-6 months of age, was considered bad for the young cat's growth, and the best time was thought to be after the female's first heat, and after the male begins spraying scent. Today, veterinarians usually want to operate before sexual maturity, even before any sexual behavior appears. The long-term effects of early operation on the male are still unproven, but most vets feel that the benefits outweigh any yet-to-be established drawbacks.

Adult cats, if operated on, continue for a long while to show signs of the sexual behavior which their surgery was supposed to remove, that is, females show some indications of being in heat, and males still spray scent and look for fights. Kelsey-Wood writes 'this is because certain behavior patterns, once established, especially in males, are very powerful and not easily changed. They have become internalized reinforcers, by which is meant that the act (i.e., fighting) reinforces the pattern. The fact that a male's sexual urges may recede does not remove its patterns of aggressiveness (willingness to fight) with other males for quite some time.' Desexing is recommended when the cat is about 4-5 months old. Some vets prefer the male to wait a month or so longer until his testicles are properly descended. There is no basis for fearing that castration will stunt growth, adversely affect skeletal development, or characteristic traits (other than making the cat less aggressive which we all want). The operation is an uncomplicated routine for a good veterinary surgeon. As for human patients who undergo surgery, the cat, too, must fast. For cats, that's about twelve hours before surgery. Although the operation does not take long, your vet will no doubt prefer you to leave the cat with him for a few hours. This is so he can check that the cat is coming round from the anesthetic all right and that there are no problems in the way of excess bleeding. Here's what happens on the operating table: The tom's testicles are removed, and many vets sew up the surrounding empty scrotum so skillfully that the cat can keep right on carrying a sign (although an empty and useless one) of his manhood. The queen undergoes an abdominal incision (which surgeons are making smaller and smaller now, thanks to improved techniques), through which her ovaries and uterus are removed. With the male, there are no outward signs afterwards that the cat has been operated on. However, depending on the skill of the vet, the female will usually have an area of fur shaved. The better the vet the smaller the area—though the shaving may be done by an assistant, and some remove more than is really necessary. It's no problem, but it takes a few months for all the hair to grow back. Sterilization, that is, the interruption of the fallopian tubes (or oviducts) in the queen, or the spermatic cords in the male, is much more complicated and really senseless. Hormonal production goes right on uninterruptedly, so the cats continue to exhibit their usual sexual behavior...exactly what we're trying to prevent, though of course they cannot actually produce any offspring. It's best to leave your postoperative patient in its basket or carrying case in a

quiet room until it awakens. At that time keep a close watch on it for several hours. Most cats look for a quiet spot and sleep off their anesthesia hangovers in a few hours. In other cats, however, the enterprising spirit wakes up much faster than their senses and limbs. Those cats have to be kept from doing themselves any injury. They may attempt to clamber up stairs and fall from these, or they will try to drink and fall face forward into the water bowl. They are best placed in a room where there are no dangers. Keep inside-outside cats at least two days before letting them go outside again.

Today, in general, surgical suture threads dissolve away on their own in about a week. It's very important to observe your patient more carefully than normal during that immediate postoperative phase and to immediately contact your vet if there are any irregularities. Everything goes perfectly well in 99% of cases.

SEXLESS LIFE IS LONGER AND BETTER

The altered cats, which is how they are described for exhibition purposes, keep some remnants of their former sexual behavior. When Ophelia first came into heat, Mao (who had been altered) played out the whole nuptial ritual, including the grand finale when he mounted her and gave her the careful bite in the neck. At that point he sort of lost track of the whole idea, threw me a look that seemed to say, 'There was something else more about that, wasn't there?' and, visibly embarrassed, walked away.

Even spayed females exhibit faint indications of being in heat. They coo in a characteristic way, act particularly affectionate and turn their hindquarters towards your hand when you pet them. All assertions that castrated toms and spayed queens become fat and lazy can safely be relegated to other myths. Cats that grow portly owe that not to any misdeeds of their own but to their human companions, who pay too little attention to them...and feed them too much. It should be noted that some owners would dispute this, especially in respect to cats neutered after full maturity, and would state that the *possibility* of this happening (weight gain) is another good reason to neuter a cat while it is young.

Expert opinion on the value of castration is unanimous. The cats are, as a rule, healthier, and their fur is in better condition. They are more domestic, more affectionate, and tend to stray less. They show more interest in their human companions. Many injuries are avoided in cats that go outside; they don't fight as much. Queens are free of gynecological ailments like teat inflammation and uterine conditions, which often afflict older uncastrated females.

A mother cat and her litter. The matter of breeding requires much time and effort on the part of the owner. Additionally, it is the owner's obligation to find good homes for any kittens that he doesn't keep.

Breeding

I hope that I have, to some extent, clearly presented why you should protect your cats from the perils, afflictions and predicaments of sexuality, and why you shouldn't necessarily increase the number of cats in the world. But it may be that you have not followed the advice but intended to. During this period of delay you suddenly realize that Queenie is getter rather portly, and you have not been feeding her any different than usual. She is pregnant, so now you need to know the course of events to come. Alternatively, you may have purchased a purebred with the intention to breed with her and need to know how you should best go about this. If this is so, I hope you obtained a very sound example of the breed because there is little merit in breeding with a mediocre specimen—there is no shortage of them around. A potential breeding queen need not be an outstanding show winner, but she should not display glaring faults, poor color, or a mismarked pattern in the breeds in which this is of some importance. Once your queen shows any signs of 'calling,' you must be on your guard. You must be sure she is not let out; otherwise she will quickly find a suitable admirer—of which there will be many in your locality. If she should escape your home and is away for a period of hours,

it might be as well to take her to the vet. He or she can terminate the estrus and remove the risk that she was mated. You will then need to wait until her next estrus in order to proceed and have her mated. This will not be very long if it is during the spring and summer months.

THE STUD

The choice of stud should be made with care. For a maiden cat, he should be an older, thus experienced, tom. It will be altogether more convenient if he lives within about a sixty-mile radius or so, which will reduce your traveling time. This said, you should never choose a stud based on convenience but on whether or not he is suited for your female. The queen always goes to the stud and remains with him for a few days. When the stud owner is satisfied that your queen is ready to be mated, the two are placed together. If you are especially interested in developing a sound breeding program, it will be important that you study the subject of genetics, which has direct application to the offspring in relation to structure, colors and inherent resistance to diseases. This also necessitates the study of the various ancestors of the stud and the queen for at least three generations. Without these matters attended to, any breeding you perform is strictly hit or miss—not planned. Do not concern yourself with ancestors beyond the third generation, as their importance genetically is minimal. If their virtues have not reached the third and second ancestral generations of the stud and the queen, then they simply are not going to, because they are not present.

THE MATING

The tom and queen are placed near to each other but with a divider between them. He holds his tail high, struts up and down, and rubs his head up against the wire divider screen. When the queen begins to coo, that is, a rumble down in her throat, it's time to let the lovers meet. She'll play hard to get at first, but after

After a long wooing session, the tom can risk mounting the female. Afterwards, he'd better get away before she "thanks" him with a paw slash.

It is important that the stud has been checked by a vet for feline leukemia and has a certificate to state he tested negative. He must also be up to date on his vaccinations. Of course, your female must also be in the same state, so do be sure these matters are attended to in advance. It would be wise to let your vet give the queen a physical checkup about 14 days before she is due to come into estrus.

giving her intended mate a few paw slaps in the face, which he is quite used to, she will allow herself to be mated. This is a bit of a violent affair because the male grabs her by the neck and then unites with her. As proof that he's achieved his purpose, the queen utters a characteristic sound that you've never heard from her before. At the same moment, the tom jumps off of her back, she takes a swipe at him with her paw, and hisses at him. That's not female malice, but instinctive reaction to pain. The end of the tom's penis is provided with thorns, or spikes, which certainly don't cause any pleasant sensation in the vagina. This stimulation, however, is necessary to trigger a complicated physiological process that leads to ovulation in about twenty-four hours after the cat has mated. Cats are thus known as induced ovulators. Despite the painful experience, the queen continues to exhibit the signs of being in heat, such as being provocative and cooing. That stimulates the tom to mount her a second, a third or numerous times. They are left alone until they finish, for that naturally increases the chances of fertilization. The queen will usually wear the tom out rather then the reverse! In most cases, the tom and queen do what they have to do at their first rendezvous. If not, you have no legal claim to a second try, even though a fee has been paid. Most stud owners, however, are so proud of their stud that they will propose a second attempt at fertilizing your cat if they are informed the maiden is not pregnant. After the mating, it is important that the female is not allowed out of your home until you know she is pregnant. Unlike dogs, the female cat is able to carry the offspring of two or more males if they each mate her while she is on 'call.' Normally, if a mating is successful, the female will reject further advances from studs, and breeders often use this as an indication of fertilization.

THE EXPECTANT MOTHER

In a few weeks you'll know whether you can count on offspring. Her belly swells, and the teats stand out clearly. Most cats are more affectionate and attentive during this period than at other times. They clearly look for closer proximity to their human companions. Count on birth of the litter from day 62 on following the visit to the stud. Even an additional week would still be no cause for worry. If it lasts longer than the 62 days plus a week, however, you definitely have to take her to a vet.

You should visit the vet anyway if this is the first delivery for the mother. The expectant mother looks for a suitable spot some days before delivery. You can offer her a box or basket with sides as low or flattened down as possible. But there should be a small lip to prevent the kittens crawling out until they are old enough to do so. The bottom of the box or basket should be lined with material that's not too soft, say a seat cushion or a folded blanket, with a layer of newspapers over it. Cat deliveries are somewhat bloody affairs, and newspapers are not only relatively sterile but also absorbent. A few rags or cloths, too, are useful because the new mother likes to gather together a cozy little nest.

Show your cat this

maternity ward, placed in an undisturbed a spot as possible, even in a dark corner, and the chances are that she'll accept it. If she tries it out by lying down in it and pulling at the bottom layer one way or another to adjust it, you've won. In other cases, the expectant mother independently relies upon her florid imagination and finds her own spot. Someone I know inadvertently left a drawer open all day, exposing her finest silk dressing gown. When she came home in the evening she saw that her cat had considered that silky paradise just the perfect place to deposit her new kittens. Clothes closets, broom closets and book shelves all serve the mother cat as quiet, easily guarded sites for her kittens.

THE BIRTHS

Many kittens are born in secrecy out of sight and often at night, thus sparing the cat's human companions any anguish. You may only have to look into the cat's maternity box or basket one morning and simply admire the gifts magically bestowed upon your household. Other cats seem to place importance on their owners presence, meowing and restlessly running about to give a hint of the coming event. Signs such as exudates from the genitals may also occur. If the expectant mother is running about nervously, jumps in and out of her box,

The young are born in a membrane, which the mother licks off. Then the new kitten gets its first "cat wash."

BREEDING

and follows you around like a puppy, then you have to devote time and wait out the impending event with her. She may even want to be petted throughout the whole process; then you have to do that for her.

You'll be surprised how fast and suddenly kittens are born. All of a sudden, a little bundle just appears between the mother's legs. She licks the birth membrane and fluid from the newborn kitten, pulls out the placenta by tugging on the umbilical cord and eats it. Then she nibbles on the umbilical cord all the way up to the kitten's belly. The mother's licking also stimulates the kitten to start breathing, like slapping a newborn baby's behind to bring it to life. Other queens in the same household, especially those who have already given birth to kittens, often help the new mother by providing nursing services, thus relieving the mother of this work. Throughout all of these events, you will do best

by standing back and only watching.

WHEN PROFESSIONAL HELP IS NEEDED

The signal to intervene is only when a cat stays in labor too long, for hours, without any kitten coming out. Now is when our earlier determination of the veterinarian's availability pays off. The same is true when a kitten sticks in the birth canal, though you can already see parts of it. Experienced breeders know how to reach in and reposition the stuck newborn into the proper position to come out easily. These breeders, however, learned it only by hands-on experience from a vet or from a knowledgeable friend. A textbook, even with the best illustrations, can't teach it to you. Besides, lay cat lovers are probably too excited under these circumstances to be of much help. So, in short, get professional help!

Finally, all the newcomers are there, and you see by the

A one-day-old kitten.

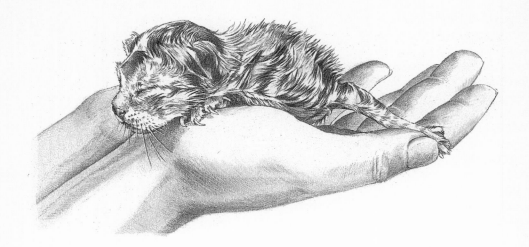

mother's actions that no more kittens are expected. Now you can count the kittens; hopefully there's no unpleasant surprise. The litter size of a domestic cat can range from one to eight, with three to five kits being the average.

To survive, a kitten must begin suckling within its first few hours of life. In a litter of more kittens than the mother can nurse, those who can't get at a teat are doomed outright.

KITTEN REARING

The mother cat helps her kittens find their way to their source of life not only by offering them her turgid, milk-filled teats but also by pushing and urging them with her paw and nose in the right direction. Since the mother doesn't like to leave the nursery during this time, it's good to place her food and water, as well as a cat toilet, near her. Most cats are good mothers and sleep only at short intervals during these first days. The rest of the time they're busy with nursing and cleaning their kittens, which they lick to stimulate intestinal activity. The mother eats the fecal matter that is produced by the infants. This first phase of intensive care lasts about three weeks, during which time the mother cat enjoys being left alone as much as possible. Visitors and admirers are certainly not welcome. Even the trusted human companion (you)

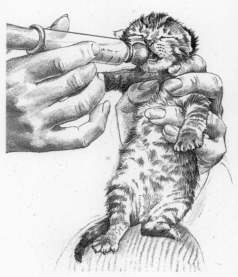

Only very rarely does a mother cat reject her newborn kitten. Feeding kittens by dropper or bottle is very arduous and must be done every two hours day and night.

usually does best by keeping some distance away. Otherwise the mother might feel pressed to move her brood somewhere else that's quieter.

A mother cat can carry her young, one at a time, over rather large distances and astonishingly great obstacles by picking up each kitten by the scruff of its neck, which makes the kitten fall into a passive transport position. I once saw a small black cat go up and down the almost vertical wall of an apartment house in Spain three times, each time with a kitten in her mouth. She was carrying her litter to the safety of the balcony of a vacant apartment because curious tourists were disturbing her where she had been under a bush in front of the house. Even at home, a mother cat can feel disturbed enough to take her brood to the most impossible hide-away

you can think of, perhaps jeopardizing her or her litter's safety.

So, exercise a little reserve and enjoy the happy new family from a reasonable distance. And it's really a pleasure to enjoy how the kittens scramble for the milk sources during those first weeks. Even now, individual character begins to show up, like bullies who always get their way by shoving their little siblings away from preferred teats. It seems as if these babies are looking for a definite teat or group of them, where they thereafter will always suckle or want to suckle. Then there's also poor little Cinderella who always gets shoved away and has to wait until all the others have had their fill. Later, this outsider often grows into the cleverest of the whole bunch because it learned the earliest in the school of hard knocks.

Kittens are born blind and

learn to see by the end of the second week at the latest. By about the fourth week, the most enterprising of the lot dare to make little trips out of their basket or box. A soft lining would be useful now so these clumsy kittens don't hurt themselves when they climb over the edge of the basket or box. By this age they will be able to eat from a saucer in a very sloppy manner. Be sure to wipe them clean when they have paddled through the food and water dish. Another cat toilet, perhaps with low sides, should be set up nearby. The mother will show them how to use it. You'll do yourself and any eventual owners of these kittens a great favor if you make this toilet as clean and convenient as possible. A kitten so guided by its mother will hardly do its duties elsewhere than in a cat toilet.

The mother now begins slowly to wean her babies. Instead of offering them only her milk as sole diet, she brings them morsels of meat from her own food bowl if they are not already eating from it, which most will be. From the sixth week on, a kitten has to fight to get a supplemental swallow of milk from its mother.

The kittens soon begin to play with their littermates and with their mother. She patiently tolerates little ambushes upon the twitching tip of her tail and also the kittens' rather reckless rough-and-tumble climbing around over her. She takes an occasional swipe, however, when the scamps let their needle-sharp milk teeth get too much out of control.

From about the fourth week on, you can integrate yourself into the cat games. In fact, you *should* do it, for this is the phase in which the kittens

The cat is a very attentive, concerned mother. At the slightest disturbance of her nursery, she picks up her kittens and moves out. The kittens offer little or no resistance in this matter.

begin to imprint on humans. The more they learn to have confidence in people, to enjoy playing with and being petted by them, the better house companions they'll make later on. Playing with the kittens also involves psychological risks. You form a bond with the little tykes, leading eventually to the question: Can't we keep *all* of them?

THE KITTENS' NEW HOMES

Although many owners with kittens will try to place them in new homes when they are as young as six weeks old, this is not advised. Such a kitten is barely weaned from its mother and is certainly not mentally or physically old enough to begin a life on its own. Very often, such kittens display what is called the 'new kitten syndrome.' They settle into their new homes really well for the first day or two and then things start to go wrong. They go off their food, start to lose weight, and very quickly succumb to any pathogens that are in the area—this is especially so during the warm summer months. Dehydration becomes a major problem because they stop drinking. Unless they receive very prompt veterinary care, the prognosis is not good at all for their survival. At this age the natural immunity to diseases they received from their mother's milk is becoming very weak, yet they have not yet received their first injections. Even if they have, these take up to three weeks to become fully operative, so

they are in a sort of 'no man's land' with regard to the resistance to disease. If they are let outdoors at this time, the situation becomes even more risky because there are more pathogens outside your home than in it. The stress of leaving mom and their siblings is a major factor in contributing to this syndrome and is heightened if the new owners do not maintain the same feeding regimen and basic style of living, which they rarely do. All of this underscores the fact that a kitten should be retained with its mother until it is 8 weeks old at the very least, while 10-12 weeks would be an even better time for you to let the kitten go to its new home. By then it is much more settled in its eating habits, should have been vaccinated, and is far less dependent on its mother for attention. If you are paying a high price for a potential show or breeding kitten, it may even be better to leave it with the seller until it is 16 weeks of age. By that time, its high-risk health period has passed, and you would indeed be unlikely to have problems, other than minor ones.

But sometimes the pet owner is too anxious to buy a tiny baby, and unfortunately there are backyard breeders who simply do not know enough about kittens to understand the importance of retaining them for those extra few weeks—which represent a very long time in feline development. By this I mean that 2-4 weeks to you seems a short period, but during that

time a kitten makes tremendous progress from a physical standpoint. Of course, some owners simply want to get rid of the kittens quickly so they do not have to pay out more money on feeding costs. But as a true cat lover, I am sure you will heed the advice that I have give you.

This mother cat is keeping careful watch over her inquisitive youngsters.

Illness and Veterinary Care

Some cat books dedicate a great deal of space to diseases and injuries. Many people who have studied up on everything from A to Z have become a sort of representative hypochondriac for their cats. They worry themselves into a dither, coming up with new symptoms at every turn.

On the other hand, there are nature fanatics who believe that nature heals animals, so we don't have to get involved in the process. You hear people say 'The cat is tough,' or 'The cat has nine lives.' That means that nature often operates in a grim way: she usually lets sick animals in the wild die or be killed by predators. But we want to save our sick or injured cat, without continually inventing illnesses it doesn't have. I'll try to point out the way of moderation between over anxiety and lack of concern.

The cat is naturally endowed, and quite amply, as an extremely viable and resistant predator. Some injuries, particularly external coat and skin wounds from cat fights and rough branches, clear up relatively easily, needing only cleaning and covering with a suitable antiseptic lotion, powder, or ointment. Cats are not so resistant to infectious diseases, however. Cats developed as animals of the steppes and of the desert, which are relatively germ-free environments. That is, however, only an opinion that has not yet been scientifically proven.Don't let all this talk of illness darken your hopes. Well-kept cats seldom get sick. Well kept means that they have access to veterinary care. They don't have to be overdoctored or protected from every draft of air, like the lady did in whose home I almost suffocated until I opened a window despite the presence of her cats. Cats living continually under controlled air conditions are perhaps more susceptible to respiratory conditions. Just how resistant cats are to temperature fluctuations is demonstrated by cats who dash out into a snow storm directly from their warm spots under a radiator and are none the worse for it.

So you don't really have to worry too much when you live with your cat in our dynamically integrated way. You'll soon note when the cat is actually sick. Living in close proximity soon alerts you to any unusual behavior, like crawling off to suffer alone and silently in some corner, instead of taking the usual nap in the accustomed niche. It would be a very unobservant owner who doesn't notice that. When your cat doesn't magically appear at the usual times, and so on, you may be witnessing a symptom, indeed a serious one. If it keeps up, see the vet.

Any amateur diagnosing and therapeutic efforts may be absolutely off track. Even the vet, who is well schooled in dealing with non-speaking patients, will in many cases offer merely a presumptive

cat's cough clears up after antibiotic therapy, then the cat had a bacterial respiratory condition. However, in countries like the USA in particular, vets today will prefer to conduct blood, fecal and other tests on ill patients. Whether such tests are really needed as often as is suggested by a vet is a moot point, but with high-tech equipment now very much a feature of the modern veterinary clinic, its cost must be justified by using it!

The right vet is important for the beginning cat owner. Once you've found him, leave all the unpleasant procedures to him. It's better for your cat to fear him than to fear you.

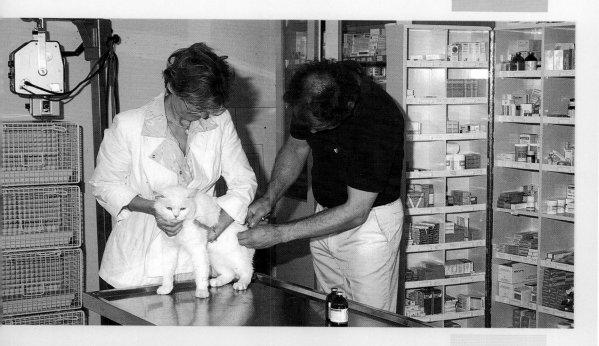

diagnosis based upon symptoms such as loss of appetite, fever, coat and eye characteristics, discharges, diarrhea, and so on.

The vet may simply prescribe, without any great diagnostic pronouncements, medication...leaving the diagnosis for afterward. If the medication helps and the

The hardest part of practicing animal medicine is that the animal can't tell us exactly where it hurts. We can only guess based upon seeing the cat flinch or otherwise react when we touch the affected part. I recently read about headaches in a cat book, and I've been wondering ever since whether a cat that pulls away in apparent pain when petted has a headache, a toothache, or an earache?

HOW TO FIND A GOOD VETERINARIAN

It's better to go once too often to the vet than once too little, assuming, of course, that we've found a vet to our liking and in whom we have confidence. He or she should not only be professionally competent but also an animal lover who knows our kind of animal as an individual and not just another case to be processed through the animal clinic.

Fortunately, being a veterinarian is more a labor of love than being, say, a physician for human patients. I don't know of anyone who studied veterinary medicine because he had straight A's in high school and college, or because his father had a flourishing practice. The latter may certainly happen, but in those cases the vet generally grew up in close contact with animals, when love and compassion for animals were instilled during childhood...which is something we cannot automatically expect of the offspring of human physicians and surgeons.

As so often is the case, the recommendation of a person we can trust is the easiest way to find a good vet. You'll hear how that vet acts in one situation or another, and also in general. You'll also find out just how available that

particular vet makes himself when it's unpleasant or inconvenient to render his services. Then you can try him out on a few routine calls: shots, vitamin injections, and later, castration. All of that will reveal something of the vet's competence, attitude, and the whole style of his practice. Even the way his assistants perform is indicative. If he's interested in our cat(s) and treats both patient and owner decently, we can invest some trust in him or her.

When recommendations are not available, you must proceed with the trial-and error-method. Some vets are very dog biased, or they specialize in horses, so you need to find one that attends many cats. Some vets have a natural ability to ease your worrying mind; others are rather standoffish in their attitude. This makes them no less a super vet, but it is human nature that we want to deal with a vet who treats us, and our cats, more as friends than one with whom we do not feel relaxed. The former you will trust, the latter you may not, even though he or she is the most honest vet in the area. It's akin to 'bedside manner' in a doctor: some have it, some do not.

AVOID DO-IT-YOURSELF TREATMENT

I've steadfastly held the belief of letting a vet do the whole job when unpleasant procedures are involved. And almost all procedures that affect a cat's freedom of movement are unpleasant. All legends to the contrary, a sick or injured animal doesn't realize that you are only trying to help it. All therapeutic interventions and procedures, taking temperature, injections, and so on, involves subjecting the poor cat to violence (at least as the cat understands it). Even during petting and playing, a cat takes a dim view of being held tightly or immobile, so it really objects much more when something uncomfortable always seems to happen after being restrained.

If the cat receives the unpleasant handling from its human companion, or in his or her otherwise trusted presence, the relationship of trust and confidence between this human being and this cat is adversely affected; the cat can be confused and aggressive. Most of the vets I asked shared my opinion: they prefer to treat their patients in their own clinics and with their own assistants. There's a desirable side effect: the strange surroundings, dogs and cats, keeps your cat subdued, timid, making it easier to handle. It's understandable that many cats break out in loud complaint at the mere sight of white coats, and that certainly pains the animal lover part of the vet. It hurts me, too, whenever I have to use any force on my cats. So I'd rather the pain be in my wallet, for frequent visits to

the vet do add up, though I tend to be rather conservative in any recourse to vets.

Some vets even have a piggy bank into which the better of animal lovers can leave a donation now and then as a kind gesture towards the treatment of pets owned by poorer people. If I were retired on minimal finances and had to bring my cat to the vet, I'd most likely ask about this fund or kitty.

Once again, I make it a rule to stay as far as possible in the background when I bring my cat(s) to the vet. I like it best when I can deliver my cat in its carrying case to the door of the clinic, and then pick up the treated cat there later on. Like that, the cat doesn't associate me with its unpleasant experience, is happier than ever to see me, and even more affectionate than otherwise.

In some emergencies, and also when the veterinary assistants are not available, the veterinarian may need our help. They will show us how to restrain even a strong cat on the table. You and the vet both have to be on your toes to protect yourselves from your cat's active resistance.

It's obviously better to prevent than to heal. I'll discuss the diseases for which a cat can be vaccinated or inoculated but first we'll mention only the vaccinations, the most important of which is a combination one against feline distemper. The first dose is given about the eighth week and the second one in another two weeks; that sequence is repeated every year. This disease is also known as feline panleukopenia or feline infectious enteritis.

Whoever has lost a cat to feline leukemia will be glad to hear that a shot is now available to immunize against it. Leukemia, once publicly referred to as cat AIDS has only one thing in common with its human counterpart: it involves a deficiency in the immune system, often causing the cat to suffer one

Cats have to be stopped from licking large wounds and skin eczemas, or they'll continue to re-infect themselves.

disease after another until it dies...a painful sequence both for the cat and its human companion. It is futile to vaccinate a cat against leukemia unless it has tested negative, so your vet will attend this first, then give the vaccine if the cat is free of this multiple of diseases. It is thus one of the more costly preventions. But it is worth that cost because an unprotected feline can so easily contract the disease from a carrier cat that it may meet while outdoors. Whether shots should be given against

rabies depends upon local conditions, something your vet will know about. You cannot vaccinate against this disease if you live in Britain because that country is free of the disease, as is Australia, New Zealand, Hawaii, Eire and certain oceanic islands. In each of these countries there are very strict quarantine regulations to ensure that infected pets, or wild animals, cannot arrive in them. There is a group of respiratory diseases which are collectively known as cat flu. They are especially dangerous to kittens and you can gain protection from them in a single vaccination which can also include protection against feline panleukopenia. The disease known as FIP, meaning feline infectious peritonitis cannot be tested for, nor can it be treated once the cat has it. The safeguard is via intranasal vaccine in the form of drops, so no injection is involved. This vaccine protects the sinus tissues and prevents spread of the disease to other parts of the body.The cat must be 16 weeks of age for this vaccine.

SIGNS OF ILLNESS

Even the best cared for cat can get sick. The more familiar you are with your cat's normal behavior, the more readily you can spot problems in time. In principle, any change, especially a sudden one, may indicate a health problem.

When an otherwise lively animal suddenly begins to sit around apathetically, seems to be sleeping all the time and avoiding contact, then you've got a danger signal. The head, too, may hang down, the fur can be ruffled and dry looking, and the gait unsteady. The opposite behavior, too, can indicate that something is wrong: continuous meowing and running around excitedly.

You can't really confuse the abnormal with the normal. Even an energetic cat may run down and rest a while, but once you know your cat, you'll know its normal rest from its sickly moping around. The eyes are a good indicator. If they're running, or cloudy, or if the eyelids droop, and the normally hidden nictitating or inner eyelid is visible, then some disease or condition is most probably building up. The cat's nose is not as much an indicator of health and disease as the dog's is; however, a cat's nose is usually cool in a normal state of health, so any warming up, especially along with increased discharge, could call for some concern.

Any changes in the mucous membranes of the mouth, and any off color of the normally pink tongue are symptoms that need to be evaluated. A cat's breath is, as with all carnivores, not particularly pleasant, and in gastrointestinal conditions it becomes putrid enough for even the layman to detect. A cat's fur is a good indicator of its health. If, despite usual care, it thins out or gets particularly ragged looking, then something is wrong.

Such symptoms can be associated with parasitic infections or infestations like worms or fungi, or a serious internal condition. Diarrhea, constipation or nausea can be entirely transient and harmless, as with us, or they can indicate disease. You just have to keep alert and use common sense. If a cat regurgitates the undigested

It's superstition that cats "lick their wounds or skin damage clean." In the interest of healing, "torture" instruments like this collar are used to prevent licking.

food it wolfed down just five minutes before, you needn't be concerned; it's only a natural regulatory mechanism that, so to say, compensates for the cat's gluttony. The same holds for regurgitation of grass mixed with mucus and hairs, a self-cleansing mechanism we'll come back to later. Yellowish mucus or blood mixed with it, however, is a danger signal.

You can keep aware of the cat's fecal matter and urine as you clean the cat toilet every day. A cat generally produces firmstools. At times, however, the excreta can be diarrheal, such as when the cat drinks too much milk, but it clears up in a few days after the milk ration is reduced. If the diarrhea continues, however, with two or three watery stools a day, or with blood mixed in, take the cat to the vet at once. With constipation, too, you can wait a little while and try to remedy it with more milk or with a dose of pure vegetable oil. If that doesn't work, go to the vet.

The urinary process is somewhat more complicated because you can't really monitor that as well. If you don't find any indication of urine in the cat's toilet for two or three days, a veterinary examination is called for. Traces of blood can be a sign of a serious bladder condition.

The body temperature is another important indicator of a cat's health. A cat's normal temperature is about 38.5C (101.3F), which is somewhat higher than in human beings (37C or 98.6F). Taking temperature is one of the veterinary procedures that a cat owner has to do himself. You can't run to the vet for every suspicion of a health problem. There are special thermometers, but you can also use human ones, the oral ones with a fine tip. Lubricate the thermometer tip with a little Vaseline and insert it into the cat's anus. A really tame cat hardly notices it if you pet it during the procedure. A

different patient may require two people to take its temperature: one to hold the patient and one to insert the thermometer. Temperature can vary two or three tenths of a degree (38.2 to 38.8C) just as with human temperatures. Anything above or below that is a sign of disease or illness.

DISEASES AND ILLNESSES

In general, a cat can get all the conditions that we get, though the causes may differ. That includes the common snuffles, pneumonia, bladder stones, hepatitis and malignant tumors, that is, cancer. In most cases, the vet can provide as effective therapy as the human physician can. For example, almost all bacterial infections can be well controlled with antibiotics. On the other hand, only preventive vaccination can help against viral conditions such as feline distemper, cat flu, leukosis, etc. If these diseases break out, they are often fatal because there is no specific treatment for them.

I don't want to bore or frighten you with any long list of diseases. There are special books on feline diseases, but I don't consider them very useful because they don't give the layman much to go on therapeutically; such books describe ghastly symptoms, followed only by highly technical words and advice: go to the vet! The fact of the matter is it doesn't make much difference what your cat's disease is called, just as long as your vet can cure it. There are some diseases for which there is no cure but for which treatment can enable your cat to lead a more or less normal life. Diabetes is an example of such a disease; the diabetic cat can be managed at a normal metabolic level with insulin, administered at home by daily injection. I'm convinced that here, too, as with human patients, very convenient dosage forms will be developed, such as a painless pressure injection (through the unbroken skin).

POISONING AND ACCIDENTS

Poisoning is a particularly critical subject and represents a considerable number of cases in the practice of veterinary medicine. Almost all kinds of pesticides (insecticides, rat bait, etc.), paints, wood treating substances, and even household cleansers, can endanger cats. Obviously, every kind of rat and mouse poison is a danger to cats, and can even kill them. In effect, cat owners have to run their households just as they would have to do if infants and small children were present: keep hazardous substances out of reach. You can't, of course, keep your cat from sniffing or even licking the neighbor's freshly painted fence. The saying 'curiosity killed the cat' is unfortunately often all too true. Otherwise I simply cannot understand how even a fastidious cat that scorns only mildly smelly food in its

own dish can suddenly dig into a rotten herring...the kind of bait that both official and private rat controllers often use to hold their deadly poisons. When we recently had a house painter at work, it wasn't easy to keep our cats from lapping up rainwater from a can of leftover paint, even though their water bowls were full. I had to arrange a cat protection agreement, with the help of several bottles of beer, whereby the house painters kept all buckets and containers carefully closed when not in actual use.

Symptoms of poisoning are usually spectacular enough to send a cat owner rushing to the vet...and the sooner the better. A poisoning victim can often be saved. Sometimes you may need to make the cat vomit, but at other times this is not advised. The only way you can determine what is the favored course is if you know what the cat has eaten or has on its fur that has been licked off. Unfortunately, this is rarely the case so the only procedure is to get the cat to the vet as quickly as possible.

Even the most skilled of climbers may take a false step and take a fall. An accident like that is often due to the nature of the surface being climbed or jumped upon, and not to any lack of your cat's skill. When a dry branch snaps or a board tips over, no amount of sharp claws and perfect body control helps: the cat falls with the branch or board. Falls from relatively low places can, perhaps surprisingly, be more dangerous than from a few feet higher. This is because a cat needs a certain falling distance within which to perform its legendary act of spinning and landing safely on all four feet.

Even in falls from greater heights where the cat manages to right itself, the nature of the ground can cause injuries such as dislocations, sprains and fractures. In these cases, too, the sooner you get to the vet, the better. A simple manual manipulation can often correct a dislocation, and immediately fixated fractures heal amazingly fast. The main thing with broken limbs or shock from falls is to keep the cat calm and immobile by wrapping it carefully in a blanket, or placing it onto a make shift stretcher for transportation purposes.

THE WARRIOR CAT

Then we have the beaten up cat that lost to a neighboring bully. As already mentioned, cat fights are sometimes very nasty, and the loser who doesn't get away fast enough is not spared further damage. Besides the rank order squabbles of the tomcats, the females can fight quite viciously over their territories. Typical injuries after such fighting include torn ears, bites on the head, neck and face, and long scratches or gashes on the flanks, hindquarters and hind limbs, especially on the loser. Despite the cat's well-known good healing characteristics, a visit to the vet could be in order. Bites, especially, tend to become infected and lead to abscesses because the cat's needle sharp teeth inject disease causing organisms deep down into the tissues. The vet can cleanse the wound, remove the fur from around it, and apply the appropriate antibiotics and other medications.

Young cats, including tomcats, that receive a good thrashing in their first fights, often suffer shock. When my Siamese Mao lost his first duel with a larger tom, his external injuries were far from serious, but he was foaming at the mouth, apathetic and developed a high fever. A vet gave him a sedative shot that helped us for the next two days. This vet told us that he had seen losers of tomcat fights die of punctured pride, fear and fright. Though I haven't yet corroborated that in the veterinary literature, I certainly believe that it's quite possible.

PILLS AND POWDERS

Serious illness often requires lengthy treatment with long-term administration of medication. Whenever possible, I leave that to the vet to handle with injections. There are clever instructions about how to give pills or liquid medications to a cat. I've tried them all, each of which always ended in a struggle between me and the cat; the cat usually won, with the pills scattered on the floor and the liquid drops soaking my shirt. Maybe I'm very clumsy, I don't know.

Attempts to outwit the cat are more successful. Get it used to some delicacy that it's crazy about, then keep those tidbits as a rare treat...until the time comes when the cat needs medication, at which time you can add the crushed pills, or lace it with the medicine drops. I've also successfully hidden medication in whipped cream and even in deep sea crab meat. It is often best if two people tackle pill-giving time, one to secure those dangerous raking front feet, maybe by wrapping the cat in a towel, while the other opens the cat's mouth and drops in the pill. They should hold the mouth shut, lift the head slightly, and stroke the throat gently to induce swallowing. It sounds very easy doesn't it. Its quite amazing how just a few pounds of feline fury can prove too much for a couple of hefty humans to hold onto!

This mother cat and her baby exhibit every outward appearance of good health.

Feeding Your Cat

No one wants to be disturbed while eating, and that goes for cats, too. The clear threat expressed here says this cat is not about to share even a crumb.

For good health, a cat needs a balanced diet of mainly animal protein, some fats and carbohydrates, minerals, trace elements and vitamins. In the wild, a cat gets all that when it eats its prey along with the intestinal contents and cereal grains and grasses. A purely meat diet is not adequate. Likewise, fanatical vegetarians will fail in their efforts to nourish their cats exclusively on vegetable matter. Cats need certain animal amino acids that they, unlike humans,

cannot produce in their own bodies. Besides, I think it would be terrible to deny an animal the food for which it was evolved to eat: Carnivores eat meat, which is why they are carnivores.

FEEDING A BALANCED DIET

Cats used to get the leftovers from human meals and still do in some rural and farm households. I remember clearly how my grandmother filled her Minka's bowl with spaghetti or with meat gravies. I've also seen how nice little old ladies fed the street cats around the Roman Forum with spaghetti and tomato sauce. The cats ate it because they were so hungry. We can assume, however, that my grandmother's Minka as well as the Roman cats also found more appropriate food by hunting for it; otherwise they would have hardly survived.

You would have to turn your kitchen into a laboratory in order to produce a really balanced diet for cats. You certainly couldn't do that, but the manufacturers of cat foods can. They employ veterinarians, biologists, chemists and nutritionists to develop a range of cat foods. I've met several of these specialists, all of whom owned cats and fed them with their own products. That really gives you confidence. Even at the risk of falling victim to insidious marketing ploys and advertising, you won't do yourself any favor by not purchasing branded cat foods. A reliable, well-known consumer testing organization closely examined proprietary cat food. It found that all manufacturers respected their own labels by actually including all the ingredients as spelled out on the label; these ingredients were in accord with the latest nutritional findings. In addition, the quality was equally good in all brands. The evaluators noted that some of the prices varied considerably, but were not justified by the test findings. That means that the most expensive product is not necessarily better than a more moderately priced one. So, we can save money if we take the trouble to compare prices. What you should note from the label is the percentage of proteins and carbohydrates. Cheap cat foods include more carbohydrates because these are less expensive than meats.

Commercial cat foods are sold moist, semi moist, or dry. The dry form is more concentrated in energy because the water has been removed. The moist form has the advantage of covering 75% of the cat's water requirement. With dry foods, you have to make sure that the cat drinks enough. Watch the water level in the drinking bowl(s). I would never argue for exclusive feeding with dry food, though it's very clean and practical. If the cat doesn't drink enough, then there's the risk of kidney and bladder ailments. In general, I mainly use the moist food, but also small quantities in between meals as tidbits, for example, as a reward for coming in when called. Semi moist foods have never really proved especially successful, and they tend to be rather expensive.

HOW MUCH AND WHEN?

There are several opinions on how much food to give as one portion, and when to give it. Since a cat, as a rule, doesn't overeat, some experts

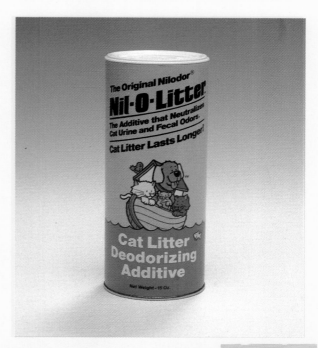

advocate the full-bowl method, whereby the cat eats at its own intervals and pace. Laboratory studies have shown that cats, given free access to food, will 'snack' as many as thirty-eight times within twenty-four hours. That's not feasible when weather or insects mess up the food. Working owners of cats are advised to feed twice daily: in the morning with enough to break the long night's fast, and in the evening to meet the rest of the day's nutritional requirements. For an average-sized cat, that's 400 grams (14oz) of prepared food. With these quantities of food, the cat stays fit and doesn't get fat. Some will eat rather less than this, others may eat more—depending on their activity level and whether they are 'topping' up with a mouse or two.

Often, however, a cat does

Nilolitter™ from Nilodor® absorbs moisture and eliminates odor from cat boxes, so litter lasts longer. Use in bird and small pet cages too.

get fat. That happens because almost every cat lover gives snacks but forgets to reduce the regular meal portions. Remnants from the table often find their way into our cats because they like to beg so nicely. And the cats don't eat the leftover vegetables but gobble up leftover gravies and pieces of meat that are too fatty, too salty, and too spicy. That can result not only in obesity but also skin eczema and loss of fur. We should really try to avoid these nutritional sins (which I, too, occasionally commit), though we've gotten away with them up to now. A certain kind of snacking is, of course, acceptable, even necessary. Cats that eat solely moist foods don't use their teeth enough. These teeth would, in the wild, be used to tear and cut into prey animals. If not used, tartar builds up on them. The tough chunks of this or that meat in moist, ready-made cat foods are too soft to really scrape off the tartar from the cat's teeth. So dry food can help do this cleansing.

It's good to let your cat have solid chunks of meat from time to time. Unfortunately, you can't take any chances today with giving your cat raw meat. There's a virus that at first came only from swine, but that now appears to also come from cattle. This disease is absolutely fatal for cats, but doesn't seem to affect swine, cattle, or human beings. A virus like that can be expected to spread like wildfire among grazing and other herbivorous animals, and soon lambs, rabbits, and fowl will most likely be affected. Fowl or poultry, of course, are already known for their dangerous *salmonella* infections. In short, meat of any kind must be cooked, and indeed thoroughly cooked, before being fed to cats.

HOME COOKING

The preceding information gives an idea of the supplemental foods you can feed your cat...but really only to keep the cat's teeth and gums healthy, or as delicacies for rewards. Also, as mentioned in the previous chapter, the delicacies can be used to disguise medication enough to get the cat to swallow it.

Besides red muscle meat like beef, pork, and veal, organ meats—heart, kidneys, lungs, liver—are useful. But organ meats should only be fed sparingly because an excess can lead to diarrhea and other problems. Most cats passionately love to eat liver. Be especially stingy with it because it contains a large amount of vitamin A, small doses of which are extremely good for cats, but excessive quantities can be somewhat toxic and can upset the absorption of other vitamins and minerals. Lung contains very few nutrients, but many cats like it. When cooked, it takes on a rather solid consistency, so it can be good occupational therapy for the teeth of overweight cats. The same holds true for heart and kidneys, though these are more nutritious. You can leave the fat on both of these organ meats if only small amounts are given; it's good for cats.

Lamb and rabbit meat are also valuable food for cats. Leftovers from the table are fine if you first carefully rinse off gravies, sauces, and spices. From time to time I cook a small chicken, which is often very economically priced, and cut it up so I can feed it to my cats over a week's time. I don't cut any of this meat too finely, which gives the cats some real jaw exercise in tearing and chewing.

BONES

The complete gobbling up of a wild bird, which would be normal for outdoor cats when they can catch one, brings me to the subject of bones. You can safely give your cat a large, smooth bone, say, of beef, with meat remnants still sticking to it. The cat would use its incisors, but especially its rough tongue to scrape off the last vestiges of meat from the bone. There's no danger of any of the bone splintering off and damaging the stomach or intestines. I wouldn't give my cats poultry bones, except for a turkey drumstick, which is very solid...although my band of roughnecks once overturned a garbage can filled with chicken bones and cleanly ate all the gristle away from them before I found out what they were doing. I don't know whether they tried to crack the hollow bones. In any case, caution is the keyword when it comes to feeding cats bones.

A water bowl is naturally part of a cat's equipment. Unfortunately, cats that are allowed outside get used to drinking from other "sources" too, whether puddles or garden ponds.

Now, a word about fish bones. Many cats love fish, while others dislike it. For cats as well as for humans, fish is an exceptional source of protein, and it also contains minerals and trace elements that appear to favorably affect the growth of the coat. I'll never forget how perturbed I was over the scrawny, unkempt stray cats I saw in Tenerife, and what a stark contrast it was compared with the cats in the next place, a small port where the native fishermen landed their catches every evening. The fishermen cut off the heads, fins, and tails of their fish and gutted them right there on the spot. A horde of about twenty cats apparently lived off of this fare. I've seldom seen such magnificent, frisky cats with such glossy coats. Over many generations, the metabolism of these cats may have adjusted to a diet of exclusively fish. They also devoured the viscera, which in many fish species contains adequate greens in the form of algae (of which seaweed is a highly nutritious example).

My cats get a fish dinner from time to time. I cook up low priced fish offal—viscera, heads, fins—from my fishmonger. The cooking, first of all, kills any bacteria and, secondly, saves me the trouble of separating freshwater from saltwater foods. Freshwater fish contain an enzyme, thiaminase, that destroys vitamin B in cats, who need this vitamin. Even a short heating up of the freshwater fish inactivates this enzyme.

Coming back to fish bones, I carefully remove them to a certain extent. It's, of course, known that many cats in the wild are skillful fishers who don't have any problem at all with fish bones. I once watched a forest cat catch a trout from a small stream and begin to eat it. I didn't disturb her but came back later to the same spot, where I found the skeleton of the trout picked completely clean...just perfect for an exhibit in a natural history museum. If I overlook any little fish bones when preparing fish for my cats, I eventually find them cleanly picked, resting on the bottom of the empty bowl.

Just incidentally, I'd like to mention that a prominent New York veterinarian reports he has clients who feed their cats exclusively on lobster, crab, and other expensive seafoods. Those cats allegedly love it. I just hope that you never buy a cat raised in a lobster household like that.

Cats are very self-willed, independent diners. 'What the cat doesn't know, it doesn't eat' is a saying that certainly fits. You can only hope that any new cat you acquire has been raised on as varied a menu as possible, and not on any specific tastes. Cats can steadfastly refuse any unusual (for them) food to the point that you begin to seriously worry about it. That can last two or three days.

On the other hand, no cat has yet starved to death in front of a full bowl of food. People usually run to the vet with cats that refuse to eat, but if nothing is physically wrong, the vet advises them to stay calm and keep trying to feed the cats.

VARIETY

You do yourself a favor when you provide a varied menu. Your cat will indicate its preferences and dislikes, so you can develop a suitable diet for it. If it gains too much weight, you can feed it less of its favorite foods for a while so that it eats less. Cats have a very fine sense of taste that is, however, mainly associated with their sense of smell. Cats that have lost this sense of smell because of disease have literally starved to death. Manufacturers of cat foods therefore enhance their products with scents and aromas, the compositions of which are closely guarded company secrets. But these will likely be based on fats, which add taste and smell to foods; they are what make foods palatable.

I used to think that the appetizing aroma that wafted out of a can of cat food when you opened it was intended to convince the cat's owner of the goodness of this brand for cats. But I eventually learned otherwise. Aroma and scent remind me of a story told to me by a former politician who came home late one night after some filibuster or other and couldn't find anything to eat except a crust of bread and a plate containing the last of a piece of canned wiener schnitzel. He gobbled up both remnants. In the morning when his wife asked if he had eaten, he said yes, and that he wouldn't mind if she bought some more of that meat since it was so tasty. But that was the rest of the cat's can! she informed him. So much for the tastiness of cat food.

Industry, constantly concerned with sales and turnover, provides us with an overwhelming line of specialty foods: cat sausage, cat delicacies, cat pastry and biscuits, and on and on. Your cat doesn't have to use all those products, but you can pamper it a bit and reward it, too, with goodies, and, under some circumstances, make sure that a passing lack of appetite isn't anything more serious than just a touch of moodiness.

For good coat and bone, cereal flakes or vegetable flakes are commercially available. Sprinkle them over the food; at least two of my cats seemed to find they were very appetizing, which makes me happy because they're my skinniest ones.

GREENS

The cat needs grass as a stomach cleanser, not as a nutrient. Experimentation in your flower pots is not what's needed here; buy some cat grass (which is often pre-germinated) at your pet shop. An inside-only cat needs it year round, and an inside-outside cat needs it only in the winter. Grass helps the cat to cough up the hair it swallowed when grooming itself. Some investigators believe that the grass tips contain minerals and trace elements that a cat instinctively looks for.

DRINKING

The cat's drink is water. As a rule, you can give it to your cat right from the faucet. In the winter when faucet water is ice cold, warm it up somewhat first. As mentioned earlier, a cat doesn't like the water bowl too close to the feeding spot. I've set up two or three watering places near the cat's favorite resting spots, such as the bedroom window sill. The water should always be as fresh as possible, changed at least once a day.

If you live in a city that has bad water, your cats may not especially like it. If it is 'laced' with a little milk, it may be more acceptable. By bad water I mean that which has been heavily treated with chemicals to make it suitable for human consumption.Unfortunately, that does not make it ideal for small pets such as cats, rabbits, birds and fish. The chloramines in it (as opposed to chlorine) are not readily removed and are generally not liked by felines. The alternative is to purchase bottled water or install a water purifier in your kitchen faucet water system, which more and more people are doing because of the terrible taste of their water supply.

Milk is not a drink for cats, all stories to the contrary. It's food, a delicacy, which many cats love, and others don't. Milk is not without its inconveniences, for many cats, particularly older ones, can't digest the lactose (milk sugar) and react especially with diarrhea as the most striking symptom. If you give milk now and then, use a kind that contains more fat, condensed milk, because the cat's digestion is more attuned to it, since cat mothers' milk contains much more fat than cow's milk. Goat's milk is also a suitable alternative to cow's milk, as many humans have found. It is easier on the stomach.

A final note about feeding is that while many cats can and do eat carrion they come across, which is surprising given how particular they can be if their high priced cat food has been down for more than a few minutes, you should not take this to indicate they can be given food that you would not eat. Sometimes your wife may take some cooked ham out of the refrigerator and sniff it. Not satisfied with its smell she may say, 'Give it to the cats because it will be OK for them'. Your feeding rule on these items should be if you won't eat it do not give to the cats either. It may not harm them—but it may not have harmed you either! If you don't want to chance it, don't gamble it on your pets either.

General Care

When in doubt or danger, have a wash—that could easily be what a mother cat will tell her kittens as one of life's golden rules! When a cat cleans itself, it makes a very entertaining scene. People find it cute, quaint, or droll, and it often shows up on corny picture postcards. Your cat is an extremely clean animal in its personal cleanliness. It is the only animal that spends so much time on body care (but rodents and rabbits would run it a close second). Long term observations showed that up to a third of the cat's waking hours is spent on grooming itself.

Grooming, however, is not only for cleanliness. It also fulfills a psychological need of the cat. Paul Gallico described it best in his charming cat story *My Friend Jennie*. I don't think any behavioral psychologist with scientific facts can surpass Gallico's intuition. In Gallico's story, little Peter, who is transformed into a cat, is advised how to act like a cat: If you're ever in doubt about anything, wash yourself. That's the first rule. If you've done something wrong and are getting scolded, wash quickly. If you lose your balance and take a tumble, wash! If you're fighting and want to break off hostilities, wash! Don't forget, all cats respect each other when

grooming. If you came into a room filled with strangers who confuse you, just sit in the middle of them and wash a bit! If someone calls you, but you don't feel like going, but don't want to hurt the caller's feelings, just wash! If you're on your way somewhere but suddenly forget where you're going, sit down a moment and freshen

The cat's care of its fur with paw and tongue takes a great deal of its waking time.

up! If anything is hurting you, wash it! If you're tired of playing with someone but don't want to hurt your human playmate, then calmly wash up! If you ever sit in front of a door and get mad because no one will open it, wash! If you get mad because someone pets another cat or a dog in the same room, don't fret, just wash!

I've experienced all of these situations. My cats wash and

groom themselves like all cats, and I have a wonderful time watching them wash out of every inconvenient, embarrassing, confusing, and painful situation.

SELF WASHING

Washing and grooming, of course, is mainly a hygienic procedure whereby the cat removes loose hair, dust or, other substances that get into the fur. In addition, licking seems to stimulate hair growth. Since cats don't sweat, the evaporation of saliva fulfills the cooling function of sweat. Cats groom themselves more often during warm weather.

Grooming starts when the cat is in its third week. Before that, the mother kept the kittens clean, and even continues to help them afterwards. Grooming appears to make the kittens feel good enough to purr, and that response remains with the adult cat. Kittens also groom each other, just as grown cats who live in the same household may do. It satisfies a social function and neutralizes aggression. When my toms Einstein and Mowgli lick each other clean, there's sometimes a tense moment when you can feel how those two are just barely repressing their biting reflex. Eventually, some biting does break out until one of them squeaks and bounds away.

The cat's grooming tools are its horny tongue and, for its face and ears, a paw moistened with the tongue. Loose hair adheres to the tongue and is swallowed. The hairs eventually form hairballs in the stomach and are regurgitated, a quite natural process, though it does look rather dramatic to see and hear an apparently choking cat. This throwing up of a hairball is made easier if the cat can eat some grass. Some hairballs pass through the whole digestive system and are eliminated in the feces, all of which is still a normal occurrence.

In longhaired cats, and in all cats (including shorthaired) during shedding times, so much hair can be ingested that it constipates the cat. In that case, a few drops of vegetable oil in the food, or feeding with foods I've mentioned to be laxative, will help.

Almost all cats love to groom themselves and like to be brushed. Only rarely do you find a cat too lazy to groom itself, in which case you try to inspire it to groom. This can be done by making its fur dirty, but pleasantly so...by smearing a bit of butter, or a little of the mush from a can of cat food on its fur. The cat at first perceives that as unpleasant and licks it away...but it tastes good and the cat likes it. Now you've conditioned the cat toward a positive response.

BRUSHING FOR HEALTH

If you regularly brush your cat, you won't have a grooming problem like the above one. Brush your cats daily, especially if they are longhaired. It's worth the

effort. You can get them accustomed to a definite time for brushing, which gives you a chance to check the cat over at regular intervals for skin or fur damage and parasites (fleas, lice, ticks, mites). Some of these can be taken care of quite rapidly. Additionally, brushing tones up the coat and helps to keep it beautiful and glossy if you follow the ladies' method of making a hundred brush strokes every day. Brushing also reduces the risk of hairballs in the cat's stomach.

How do you go about brushing a cat? With the lie of the hair, starting on the neck, then the back and flanks, then the tail. The underbelly can be done last. With medium to longcoated cats you can then brush against the lie before grooming the hair back into place. This ensures that the snags at the coat base are removed. After using the bristle brush (which is preferred to nylon because it does not create so much static electricity) you can then groom with a medium toothed comb. Be especially careful on the underbelly and on the tail, both areas of which are very sensitive. If you are heavy handed as a groomer your cat will come to hate being brushed—but done daily and gently, it will be a very pleasing occasion for it.

BATH ONLY WHEN NECESSARY

The cat's tongue and our brush will nicely take care of any dirt and soiling that can

"Washing" is particularly important during shedding, which can occur two to three times a year even in cats that live only inside the house and never go out.

usually be expected to occur at home. Cats that go outside, however, might get into tar, paint or who knows what else. In no case should you apply any solvents, spot removers or paint thinners. If the soiled spot is relatively small, simply cut it away with blunt-nosed scissors (like bandage scissors). The same method can be used when longhaired cats get a piece of twig, burdock or sandspur entangled in their coat. When extensive areas are involved and the substance cannot be removed, go to the vet. Of course, if your cat is an exhibition animal you cannot go cutting bits of hair away, so must carefully groom the hair and then bath the cat to remove any stains or dirt.

The pre-bath groom is vital if you do not want to end up with mats forming in the coat. If for some reason your cat is in a very dirty state for whatever reason, then it will need bathing, but do not do this for its own sake. When bathing a cat it is best if two people do this because, at least during the first two or three baths, cats react violently to the process. Thereafter, they get used to it if you have not made any major errors. These would be letting shampoo suds get into the eyes or ears (place cotton wool into the latter) or if you used water that was too hot or too cold. After the bathing is done be very sure to rinse thoroughly to ensure there is no residual shampoo in the hair. It could cause an irritation when it dries. Also,

shampoo left in the coat will make the fur sticky and dull in appearance. Use a special cat shampoo, or one produced for babies. Towel dry well and then keep the cat indoors until it is dry, when it should then be carefully groomed again to remove tangles caused by the toweling.

PEDICURE AT THE POST

The cat takes care of its own manicure by sharpening and honing down its claws on the furniture, which makes furniture manufacturers and upholsterers happy! That can become rather annoying, so it became fashionable for a while in America to amputate the front claws. In some countries, like Germany and Britain, vets don't perform that operation and the subject has been discussed earlier in the book.

Behavioral research has long ago shown that the sharpening of claws is an important part of their social behavior, whereby they release tensions and impress their fellow cats. Clawing is no problem with cats that have access to the outdoors. They find a tree with a rough bark, which they like much better than dad's wing chair. For cats that live exclusively inside, you will need a scratching post.

A cat may still claw furniture, however, and if you have more than one cat others might well imitate the scratcher...especially if dominance displays are involved. To discourage this

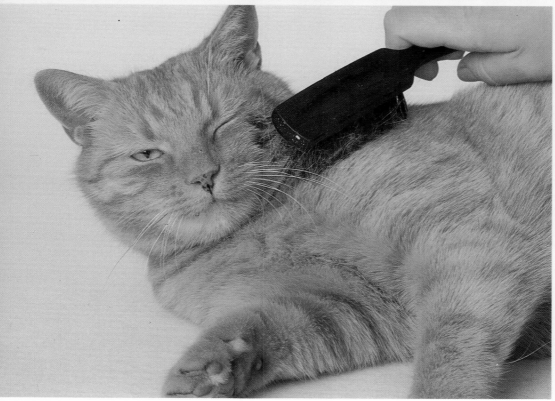

The elegance and elasticity of the cat body never stop thrilling the cat lover. Based upon human performance standards, all cats would be top performers.

you must catch them in the act and give them an energetic 'No' or shoot them with a water pistol. There are sprays to keep cats away, but the products I tried out were more like sprays to keep humans away. They stank horribly, especially right after application. In general, the cat gives itself an adequate manicure by its clawing activity. You might find something on the scratching post or tree from time to time that an inexperienced cat owner would take for a ripped out claw. Don't be concerned. It's only the outside nail casing that was pulled off.

It's a good idea to cut the claws of the inside-only cat: if you do trim, take care not to cut the bluish artery, often called the 'quick' in the claw. If you can manage to see the cat's claws, you'll still have difficulty seeing this, and where it ends. If you are uncertain about the process the best thing is let the vet attend it for you.

EAR CLEANING

While brushing your cat, have a look in its the ears. They open far forward and catch not only the slightest sound but also dust and dirt. Cats can reach only the outside parts of their ears with their paws. So we have to help sometimes. Ask your vet to show you how far you can penetrate the cat's ear canal with commercially available cotton wool swabs. If you find light brown ear wax, that's normal. If the substance is blackish, suspect ear scabies, or mange, or even mites, and let a vet attend the cleaning or supply the preparation and the instructions for you to follow. The very outer parts of the inside flap can be wiped with a dilute saline solution, which will remove surface debris and kill microscopic organisms.

CAT TOILETS

Cat toilets save a lot of worry and trouble if they're as clean as the cats themselves. If

a cat finds its toilet dirty, it looks elsewhere for a place it considers cleaner. Even if you have only one cat, two cat toilets are advisable. They have to be inspected daily, preferably twice. I advise you not to experiment with using sand, peat, paper but to stick with traditional cat litter which is made specifically for its purposes.

With commercially available cat litter, however, some experimen-tation may be worthwhile. The one I prefer is based upon a kind of clay, that clumps beautifully. Feces, urine and litter form solid dumpling-like clumps that can be easily removed without dragging any clean litter along with it. This type is more costly but works out thrifty because you don't have to change it so often. Quality litters can be flushed down a toilet because they are biodegradable. The cat toilet should be scrubbed with boiling water and rinsed with a disinfectant. Finally, rinse out with water. Now, any worm eggs, too, have been eliminated along with excrement and odor.

Don't forget to look for anything that wiggles in the

Concern yourself only with the outer ear if and when you clean them. Going any deeper is not only not useful but can even injure the cat. Be careful!

Cat toilet sanitation is the whole story in cat cleanliness and hygiene.

cat's daily droppings. I won't burden you with exactly what kind of parasitic worms might be present...just go to the vet if you see anything wiggling in the kitty litter. The cat toilet might smell a little of antiseptic after its weekly cleansing, an odor that certainly won't bother the cat once fresh litter is placed in the tray. I recently met a cat owner who said that a cat toilet had to smell with a natural odor so that cat could find it again. That's the kind of household where every sniff you take makes you exclaim 'It smells like cats in here!' Such a toilet is more likely to put the cat off rather than to use it. If the cat knows where its toilet is, that is the main thing (as it is with humans). Perhaps these other sort of people like their human toilets to smell so their guests will know where it is when they want to use it! Some people really do have so very outdated notions about cats.

CAT GAMES

Cats, like all mammals actually, enjoy playing games. These are important to them in helping to establish their place in hierarchies, or as early training in survival techniques. For cats, as predators, the games they like best are those based around stalking and leaping, and using their claws to attack objects. They enjoy

A stable cat tree is an ideal playground for several cats. Here, they can scratch and climb to their heart's content. Hiding niches and resting platforms, too, come in use.

throwing things in the air and then using their lightening reflexes to catch the object with their paws as it descends back to earth. The following are a few suggestions for you of objects and games to play with your cat. The time for this play in the evening is well spent. I wouldn't know what could be more relaxing and better against stress after a hard day at the office or other workplace. In this regard, we can refer to objective, scientific studies that indicate a relationship with cats is associated with a significant drop in blood pressure, and changes in skin and muscle tone. To be fair, the same is true if you keep horses, dogs, rabbits or other pets. Even tropical fish as a hobby offers advantages, such as reduction in stress levels. How you play with your cat develops over the course of time. Cats let you know what they like. They are highly individualistic in this respect, too. What is a great success with one can't raise any interest out of another. Sometimes a cat suddenly loses interest in a previously well-liked game. It becomes too boring for the cat. Then you have to try variations of the game, or simply invent a new one. That keeps your imagination bubbling.

Because of the scope of this variation, I haven't limited myself to only my own experience, but have interviewed many people about their cat games. Here are the results: All young cats like the toy mice available at pet shops whether or not they've seen their mothers capture real mice. Many prefer soft, rubbery mice into which they can sink their sharp little teeth, while yet other kittens like mice of various kinds of fur. Squeaking mice and wind-up mice that scurry about can often trigger sheer panic in kittens, but this quickly turns to the chase when kitty realizes the that little mouse can't actually hurt it.

It's funny, or perhaps even logical, that the same goes for cat toys as for children's toys: the simpler the better. The child's or cat's imagination, respectively, does the rest. That's why all cats like balls of all kinds up to the size of tennis balls. Or you can make your own from tinfoil or other crackling or rustling paper. Then you just have to make it move effectively over the floor. A cat will run enthusiastically after it, catch it, perhaps toss it up into the air like a real live prey animal, and finally bring it to you. People who don't have cats really don't know that cats love to carry things. We cat lovers know it...often to our regret. We'd often like to stop the games and get on to other activities, but there sits a cat in front of us holding a ball nicely between its forepaws; it looks at us with cocked head, and meows an invitation to play...and we let it roll for the tenth time.

This game keeps cats young. Even our senior cat Ophelia, who was almost seventeen years old, was always ready to hobble behind any rolling round object. Many cats like to play hide-and-seek games with you. They place themselves in front of you, perhaps in a sort

the big bad cat? Then he races away from me, coming around to attack me (with retracted claws) from the rear. Childish? Yes, I admit it.

A favorite game is for the cat to hide under an

of threat stance, the tail bent, then they dash off, and you're supposed to follow. They hide somewhere, and they'll be happy if you don't find them at first. Suddenly they pop up again, and you really wouldn't be surprised to hear them exclaim 'Aha! Gotcha!'

These hide-and-seek games are, of course, replete with expressions that are as ritualized as possible, such as 'Now where is that cat? I can't find the cat!' After some practice, you can trigger the game at will. For Einstein and me, we call the game Are you

overhanging piece of sofa cover, bedspread, or tablecloth, where it waits for you to tap on it. A paw will shoot out to hit your hand. Careful! The needle sharp claws will usually be exposed and ready for use, presumably because no visual contact inhibits the cat, who would otherwise take more care of the hand that feeds and pets it. Cats generally realize that bare human skin doesn't tolerate any sharp claws. If your cat is still getting you with its claws, try a loud Ouch or Hey

Play with your cat to keep it young longer. Thick ropes are a favorite toy. Cats will play alone with them, but it's so much nicer if you snake the rope around for them.

A ball of yarn is a classic toy for cats and appears in many paintings. The lady of the house, however, doesn't relish her yarn being clawed up. Besides, the cat gets entangled easily in the strands and can even hurt its paws.

to remind him. Some cats learn to be gentle, others never do, they are simply rough players. Cats are thrilled by packing materials of all kinds, especially those like tissue paper that rustle and crackle so invitingly. Let your cat help you unwrap packages... what I really mean is, I'd like to meet the person who can stop his cat from involving itself in his unwrapping of packages. A cardboard box with crackling paper solves the whole problem of what game to play tonight. But only tonight, for even that quickly gets boring.

You can also set up on the floor a play landscape of all kinds of paper. Clever crumpling, folding and stacking creates a labyrinth of passages, tunnels, and exits. The cat is delighted to get into it all. Now, all you have to do is to rattle the paper at different places...until a little jack-in-the-box strikes at it, then immediately withdraws. A refreshed, well rested cat won't tire easily.

If you care to trail a length of string on the floor and slowly pull it, this will see most cats, and all kittens, pouncing on it. But have care not to drag the cat when it has a hold of the string in its mouth. Another suggestion is this. Attach a length of stiff wire, such as on a motor car speed cable, from the top of the scratching post, or any other comparable height, and tie some cloth to it (only a few small pieces, butterfly size). It will dangle down under its own weight about a foot from the floor. When kitty or cat jumps and grabs it, it will immediately spring upwards and away from them the minute they release their hold. The prey has got away! The cat will then dive into action and try to capture the bobbling cloth. You can now purchase similar wire games from pet shops if you don't have a length of suitably springy wire in your home. The advantage of an extended playtime is that it keeps the cats from inventing their own games that negatively affect your furniture and other household trappings. If you don't direct their inexhaustible store of playful imagination, then they'll use it anyway. You can watch how they single out some object in the house, stalk it, and then bag their prey in one fell swoop. The urge to hunt needs an outlet, especially for the inside-only cat. If we create that outlet, then we also control it. In any case, we can console ourselves despite any damage to the household caused by over-zealous play, that our cats remained young in spirit and body, active, healthy and happy. The broken glass over great-grand aunt Rose's portrait in the antique silver frame is, after all, not so priceless that it can't be replaced.

My Siamese tom Mao and I invented a petting game, which I call sleigh riding. When Mao threw himself over on his back while being petted, I grabbed him gently with both hands under his forelegs and literally scrubbed the carpet with

him, pushing him back and forth along his long axis! He purred in pure joy, stretched his forepaws way over his head, hooked his claws in the carpet and pulled himself further ahead. In the second phase of this game, he held himself very stiff, and I took hold of his hind legs so I could push him back and forth, often for a yard or so. I was very proud of my invented game. Then I read a piece by the English writer Beverly Nicholls in which he describes a favorite game for all Siamese cats, a game that seems to be unknown even in the best of cat-lover circles. He called it back-sliding or sledding. So much for 'my' invention. The carpet and rugs used for the sleigh rides and back-sliding, of course, will need a vacuum cleaner.

Above, left: **Contrary to common opinion, cats don't like to jump from great heights. This "treed" Siamese cat goes as far as it can along the side of the cabinet before jumping...** *Right:* **...and then tries to keep contact with the side even during the jump, thus making for an easier landing.**

The Predatory Cat

At some time or other you, as a cat owner, must realize that you're sharing your home with a predator, a carnivore evolved to hunt live prey. This animal has an inborn hunting instinct that first and foremost, assures its survival. This urge to hunt, strangely enough, seems to be independent of any hunger or need for food. We know that even well-fed cats are enthusiastic, first-class hunters. Most probably, this continued drive to hunt is due to the simple fact that those little rodents that represent the cat's natural food are just snacks. Calculations show that a cat that doesn't get any other food needs about twelve little snacks like those mice a day. Very reliable studies show that only every second to fourth hunting effort is successful. So, it's easy to understand that it's very reasonable of evolution to build into a cat an urge to use every opportunity to (practice) bagging prey.

People who are horrified that nature consists to a large extent of eating and being eaten should perhaps not keep any cats. Otherwise they could be really shocked when their little pussycat suddenly turns out to be a talented, savage hunter. I had an older friend who constantly attacked my love of cats because they were mice eaters and bird catchers. He had the naive impression that there could really be a world in which the lion could eat grass in peace with the lamb. That paradise doesn't exist on earth. And what about the feelings of the grass...today when even Prince Charles speaks with his plants!

KITTENHOOD PREY

You've got to see all this unsentimentally and realistically, or you'll get so flustered and upset that you'll bog down in it. On the other hand, you can't let your cat carry out all of its predations unchecked. As natural and instinctive as it may be, we still can't simply give nature free reign. We have a way of changing nature so quickly and thoroughly that the nature of our cat can't keep up. At this point our higher intelligence has to guide our intervention. We can't allow everything that the cat catches or brings home to be its prey.

It begins quite harmlessly. Insects are usually a young cat's first prey. On some summer evening when the balcony door or windows are open, little pussycat will discover that a thick, brown moth is fluttering about its favorite lamp. Or, little Mush-Mush is sitting in the sun on the window sill, watching a huge bumblebee trying to buzz through the glass pane to escape outside. Mush-Mush's little tail starts to whip around, and a little paw darts up towards the tiny moving thing on the glass. Mush-

A calico stalks through its territory. There's no doubt that this born huntress is in her element.

Mush eventually catches the creature and makes its wings unfunctional, but it still manages to crawl about on the glass. The little cat paws and bites some more until the bee lies motionless. At that point, the cat sniffs the bee to see if it's edible. Often those things smell so foul that the cat sneezes and shudders a bit and simply lets the bagged prey lie there, uneaten. Other times, the cat cracks it open and swallows it. Some things really don't taste so bad after all. Studies have revealed that insects make up a certain proportion of the diet of house cats that live in the wild. When in need, cats will also eat flies.

My tomcat Mao once cleaned off (that is, by eating) a whole, white wall of a long legged species of cranefly or gnat, and, with apparent relish, devoured a huge moth...which made him reek of chlorophyll. My tom Mowgli acquired the remarkable habit of digging up earthworms and carrying them around. Just delightful. Along with earthworm bits and pieces, he also evenly distributes the soil from my garden beds over the carpeting and cushions on which he recuperates his energies following the earthworm hunt. Incidentally, he also seems to eat some of the earthworms he catches.

What worries me more about these little gourmets is whether the prey animals have been ingesting and storing up any pesticides or herbicides. If insecticides are used in your home, don't let your cat eat any dead or dying victims.

THE FIRST 'BIG' PREY

Sooner or later every cat lover experiences how their home tiger bags its first prey. The cat with outside

The typical hunting leap or spring of a cat: It crouches close to the ground and treads with its paws...

permission will, of course, certainly drag something home, but so will the strictly inside cat. It's amazing how many mice still continue to live in homes, especially in areas with some natural surroundings, and in ground floor apartments. Also, birds with suicidal tendencies still alight on the terraces, balconies and window sills of cat households...and fate at some time or other strikes out at them in the form of a cat paw.

Human sympathy remains under control as long as prey species, like insects and so on, are involved. But once a cute little mouse or a pitifully squeaking bird is caught, we're thrown into the serious state of having to decide upon life or death. Should we take the still viable and screeching prey animals away from the cat or not? For now begins the proverbial cat-and-mouse game.

THE FELINE THRESHOLDS

The first scientist to thoroughly investigate the behavior of cats, Professor Leyhausen, observed their hunting behaviors or thresholds. The essence of his observations was that the cat goes through a series of obligate thresholds, the highest being of killing and eating its prey. Once satiated it will still stalk, hunt, and maybe kill the prey, until that threshold is satiated. Thereafter it will stalk and maybe pounce but will not kill. The lowest threshold is that of waiting for the opportunity to stalk—which is why cats are so good at simply sitting around for long periods and observing: they are waiting for the chance to stalk. It used to be thought that this activity (the catching but not killing) could be explained by the puerilification of the house cat, who was supposed to learn its business from its mother by playing it out first, and then kept those practice antics for life as real play, since in most cases the cat didn't have to rely on hunting to live. And this misconception even caused the well-known animal encyclopedist Alfred Brehm to call the cat gruesome and cruel because it was believed to purposely torment its prey. This view was corrected when wildcats, too, were observed to carry out the same prey 'game'.

The question for the cat lover remains, however, as to whether the cat or the prey gets our support! I've solved this problem

pragmatically, with the help of experience.

The first prey that my tom Mao bagged was a careless linnet, which he caught one early summer morning on our balcony. I wasn't a witness to the tragedy and found a beak, two wings and about five million little feathers. The room looked as if pillows filled with green down had been slashed open and shaken out over the furniture and floor. After half an hour's work vacuuming up the mess, I reached my decision: I would relieve my cat of any and all birds, dead or alive. We'll talk more about alive later.

With mice, I let things run their natural course. Why?

First, it's nearly impossible to snatch a mouse away from a cat. Second, the mouse might bite you, causing a nasty infection. Third, catching mice is, in fact, part of the cat's intrinsic nature, and indeed one of the original, historic reasons why it intimately shares our lives with us.

Often, with a well-fed cat it will, after some time, lose interest in the apathetic, half-dead mouse and leaves it to its fate. Now you, as a cat lover, who is also generally a lover of all animals, are called upon to put the poor mouse out of its misery. Some people use a hard object; many even use a frying pan (as a club). It sounds grisly, but it has to be done.

RATS AND RABBITS

Protection from rodent plagues also applies to rats. Cats, at the very least, have a deterrent effect on these fellow inhabitants that share

...then suddenly jumps or takes a flying leap...and gets a mouse if lucky.

our large cities with us. The very cautious rat is a quick learner and, after the first encounter (at the latest!), avoids any home which a cat guards...if the rat survives the first encounter. A rat does indeed often survive because an inexperienced cat shies away from fighting the beast. Fortunately, only a few cats develop into rat catchers and rat killers. I say *fortunately* because even though a smaller cat can finish off an average-sized rat, it often takes a pitched battle which sometimes ends with serious injuries.

Rats usually defend themselves from cats by leaping right to the attack, aiming for the cat's face, eyes, and ears. Wounds inflicted like that can be serious and often become infected. After a rat fight, carefully examine your cat, and, if necessary, see the veterinarian. In addition, rats may transmit diseases (remember the Black Plague?) against which they themselves may be resistant. Rats, too, may simply be infested with smaller vermin—fleas and lice.

Keep in mind that your cat may have won its rat fight only because the rat was already suffering from the effects of some rat poison it had previously ingested...putting your cat in the greatest jeopardy if it were to eat any of the rat. In any case, it's somewhat of a hair-raising feeling to watch your cat bring a live rat to you in the living room. That's

a rare event, however, because a rat fight is so vicious that the cat has no other choice than to bite the rat dead, or let it go.

On the other hand, I've seen how my three hero cats just sat around a live rat and finally lost absolutely all their interest in any venting of their natural fury against rats. I cleared a path back through the garden for it...where it, strangely, met its end. In any case, it showed up the next morning dead at the foot of the garden steps. It's likewise amazing that our most dainty, elegant tomcat, Einstein, is the most successful rat catcher. Could our pedigreed Somali and Burmese be somewhat degenerated? Kelsey-Wood concurs with my own experience and states that even many tough toms that have battled with their first rat will thereafter avoid them. He states that on one occasion (rather like mine) four of his cats cornered a rat, but none dared to tackle it as it sat on its hind feet ushering threats by grinding its teeth. The matter was resolved only when his Jack Russell terrier scattered the cats and killed the rat. He adds that if you have a rat problem, get a small dog, preferably a terrier, not a cat! Even then, he adds, you should carefully inspect the dog's face for bites. Very, very rarely do our cats bag rabbits, which are not all that rare in large cities. Those caught are usually quite young and already dead when delivered home by a cat. Why that happens and also why adult rabbits are somewhat safe from cats, I learned when the neighbor's visiting grandchild brought along dwarf rabbits.

The child let his rabbit run around free in the garden, and my cats, of course, went right for it. I had the sinking feeling that it was too late for any rescue operations, but I raced down the garden stairs anyway to make some effort at least. I need have no fears for that rabbit. It thumped the ground furiously with his hind feet and lashed out mightily with its forepaws. My three side-kicks approached more out of curiosity than of any intention to bag prey. They were fully confused and in a few moments gave up any further attempts to approach this unpleasant creature. I can't imagine that any rabbit in the wild would be the slightest bit more timid than this feisty lap pet. So, to explain why very young rabbits are sometimes caught, perhaps they have wandered too far from family and burrow, gotten scared and exhausted. On the other hand, cats are braver where small guinea pigs are concerned and may kill them because the guinea pig, unlike the rabbit or the rat, puts up little or no defense if it cannot scurry to a safe haven. It also squeals loudly which seems to excite the cat more.

BIRDS

As far as birds go, we could write a whole episode about that. If there is any consternation, vexation and strained relations with neighbors and other fellow human beings over cats, then it's with committed bird lovers. These people have read everything there is to

This staid tom won a skirmish with a rat. The cat lover does well to advertise successes like this to any neighbors who are not quite cat lovers.

read about the decreasing bird population on this planet and, sorry to say, find a potential bird murderer personified in every cat. No one has ever seen the producer of an industrial exhaust gas, a pesticide manufacturer, or an over orderly nature-destroying landscape gardener with a squeaking bird held crosswise in his mouth. These people, not cats, disturb the bird population.

Cats can indeed be caught

in the act with a bird in the mouth, I have to admit. The smaller the cat and the larger the bird, the more dramatic the bird murderer. Cats seize birds by the neck even if only to keep away from the bird's sharp beak. The birds fall into a sort of carrying trance (like the kittens do), letting their wings hang down. That makes the picture of a cat holding a bird in its mouth even more dramatic.

Mao once brought me a pigeon, with which he could only barely manage to climb the garden stairs step by step. Comparatively smaller Einstein recently dragged home a seagull that was twice as large as he was, and he couldn't even force it through the cat door. I'm really not completely sure whether he even bagged this gigantic bird himself or whether he found it dead or almost dead.

All of this may sound as if I were proud of these bird assassins, but, in fact, it is indeed a considerable achievement to bag much bigger animals like that. These are, however, the absolute exception. Our city fathers, who once tried to entice wandering falcons to settle in the cities in order to get rid of the pigeons, would certainly have had nothing against the help of cats to do that job. For one thing is certain: we have really messed up nature and its bird life, and cats can certainly lend very necessary help in regulating that environment.

For example, blackbirds have found such a good food source in the environs of our affluent society that they are reproducing beyond control and, according to experts, crowding out less numerous bird species. At the same time, they show signs of degeneration. They often produce a third brood instead of only the usual two, but lose interest in raising the third one, leaving the immature nestlings, unfed, to themselves. I don't know whether a quick death between a cat's sharp teeth wouldn't be preferable to starvation for these orphans.

Most cats, as a rule, catch birds only rarely. Birds are simply too flighty for cats. I can well understand why my cats, as a rule, ignore blackbirds on the ground. The cats don't have a chance. The blackbirds seem to know it, as far as I can judge from the nonchalance with which they hop about within reach of a cat's claws. Now and then, however, a few birds do get caught because they insist on poking around in the mulch under the rhododendron bushes, which blocks take-off. Yet, these birds are still faster afoot than a solid four-legged cat in the tangle of underbrush. And to add insult to injury, the birds scold nastily as they carry out Stuka dives on my predators following their unsuccessful attempts to bag a bird. A bird can be formidable.

STOMACH CONTENTS: EVIDENCE IN FAVOR OF CATS

The allegation that cats threaten our birds has been

The darker side of the hunting cat, who can obviously not resist the temptation of this bird nesting box. A few strands of barbed wire at the base of the tree will keep cats away.

scientifically refuted by comprehensive studies of the stomach contents of dead strays. These studies were carried out in part with bird conservation groups. Bird material found in the stomachs of cats amounted to an average of 10% by weight. This percentage quantification by weight is very enlightening because a large adult blackbird, in comparison with a small mouse, really distorts the picture so that people think of cats as bird killers. The unfair prejudice against poor cats, that they're poachers or devastators of nature, is hardly erasable.

What the anti-cat people never mention in their arguments is the millions of mice and rats that are killed each year by cats. If those rodents were not killed, thus lived to breed at their known prodigious rate, the cost to humans, both in terms of annual grain lost to them, which already runs into billions of dollars, and the increase in the spread of disease, would affect the lives of us all. To combat such increases we the public, the farmers, and our governments, would have to foot the bill for massive extra rodent measures that the cat saves us the cost of, just as it did the Egyptians! The price? Yes, cats kill birds but humans destroy far more of these than cats ever will. In Africa, Australia, and other countries, birds are slaughtered in their millions by burning, poisoning and explosives in order to protect grain crops. Even so-called bird environmentalists and associations will annually kill thousands of some species in order to protect others that are threatened or actually endangered on the CITES listings, and which are being 'pushed out' of certain areas by species that are able to adapt better to that environment. Sadly, the world is not perfect (we humans have made sure of that!) and there are tradeoffs

that are unavoidable. Cats provide an incalculable service to us. Those who bemoan them would do well to remember that when they balance the books as it were, they should give the cat its due share of enormous credits, and not simply note occasional debits!

There is one special case when cats do devastate wildlife. Cats have been brought to islands where there were no cats before. The local birds had never developed any fear of cats, and were partially (and in one or two instances completely) wiped out. The cats are not as culpable as the people who took them there, and who didn't understand what they were doing to the natural balance by releasing cats on the islands in the first place.

HOW TO COPE WITH A BIRD KILLER

I once had the misfortune of owning a bird killer who was Osiris, an Abyssinian. Instinctively, I did the right thing, which I later found corroborated in one of Dennis Turner's books. He recommended taking the bird away from the cat. In about 80% of the cases I found that the bird was still able to fly, so I let it go on its way. In addition, I avoided any praise or other congratulatory talk, also what Turner suggested. Somehow Osiris got the message about the change in game rules; he never brought me any birds again. Whether he still caught them but just

didn't show me, I don't know.

If you have a cat with an extremely powerful hunting drive, it would be unconscionable to also have potential prey animals as pets. A caged, fluttering canary, a guinea pig that scurries around in its box, and a hamster that runs crazily on its exercise mill, all represent just the stimuli that trigger a cat's hunting drive. To allow your cat to sit and peer into a bird or hamster cage for hours is unkind to the hamster or bird and very frustrating to the cat—it amounts to cruelty.

Large parrots are another matter. They usually know how to teach respect to cats. I know a household in which a cockatoo really tyrannized two cats, but generally, once they have learned respect for each other, they will live their lives by avoiding each other as much as possible.

Cats Together with Other Cats & Dogs

If anyone asks what the cat's worst enemy is, the answer always comes automatically: the dog. If two people are always feuding with each other, we say they fight like a cat and dog. That shows how caught up we are in our own clichés. In the wild, canines and felines try to keep out of each other's way, or they hardly meet one another. Lions and leopards in Africa will kill wild dogs if they get the chance, and wild dogs will drive a lion from its kill if they greatly outnumber it. But generally, these two primary carnivore families evolved to keep out of each other's way, as do all carnivores. Then man brought dog and cat together. He needed both. It wasn't too hard, either, to get them used to one another. Dogs and cats, if brought up together, live well together. It's another story when a dog owner conditions his animal to go after whatever slinks, creeps or scurries: pine martens, polecats and rats, and that even includes cats that, in his opinion, shouldn't be on his grounds or hunting territory.

Dogs are apparently intelligent or teachable enough to recognize their own human family's cat and to respect it. Our neighbor's dog Lucas is a huge traditional German Shepherd who hunts (luckily with no success) all my cats. His own family's tom cat Duscha, however, he leaves unscathed, or, at most, gives him a few affectionate nudges.The emotionally moving photographs of animals the newspapers like to publish fit into this discussion, too, such as a tiny kitten cuddling up to a gigantic St. Bernard. We find that moving because such stories reflect a sort of reconciliation of opposites, incompatibilities we ourselves have built up. Such stories show really only that we can get animals used to almost anything. It's only a matter of solving a learning problem to have dogs and cats live peacefully together. Each has to learn a foreign language and learn to interpret the behavior and body language of the other, very different species. This can be acclaimed in a friendly atmosphere, free of fear.

So it's no problem at all to have puppies and kittens accept one another as friends and companions. They meet one another as naive beginners with clean slates without any prejudice written upon them. And they really can't do very much to each

In principle, there's no enmity between cats and dogs. This Fox Terrier would defend the kitten—which is a member of his home, his "pack"—even against other dogs.

other. It's also usually not very hard to get an adult of one species to accept and get used to a young animal of the other species. The adult is self-confident enough to tolerate the youngster's impertinence. Keep a watchful eye on them, of course, in case one or the other squeaks because a little tooth or claw was too sharp.

THE LANGUAGE BARRIER

Clashes between dog and cat are mostly because of misunderstandings, as is so often the case in human affairs throughout history. Dogs and cats speak different languages. Body language is particularly subject to misunderstandings. Dogs wag their tail to show friendly feelings. Cats flick their tail when excited or aggravated. The cat thinks the dog's wagging his tail means look out, you bother me. The dog thinks the cat's flicking tail means let's play. So the dog has a certain right to get angry and aggressive when his friendly efforts to approach the cat are met with a flying paw full of sharp claws.

Their vocalizations, too, may sound similar, but mean quite the opposite things. A cat's contented and friendly purring and the dog's growling as he gets angry are differentiated only after some experience. If the cat feels threatened, it rolls over on its back so it can put all four paws into a defensive posture. The dog, however, interprets that as a posture of humility, of deference to the top dog, and so becomes careless. If the cat's defensive claws now hurt him, he finds that really unfair and against the rules of the game.

Once they understand each other, cats and dogs like to play together. The favorite game is cops and robbers, or just plain chasing. When my Siamese Mao was introduced to another family's young German Shepherd, they chased each other tirelessly around us where we were sitting and talking in the living room. When Mao had enough, he jumped up on the back of the armchairs and let the dog chase around by himself. On some of his frenzied orbits, Mao reached down and tapped him playfully on the head, at which point he finally realized that his playmate wasn't racing wildly around him anymore. Do I have to mention how proud I was of the higher intelligence of my tom cat? There is, however, a certain danger involved when a very large dog is kept with cats. By its sheer weight, a heavy dog can injure, even in play, a much smaller and lighter cat. Even a playful tap with its big paw could be too much for a cat's delicate bones. Despite that, even dogs and cats with such disparate sizes can become great friends, because the cat eventually learns to keep out of its more robust buddy's hefty signs of affection. A cat is much more flexible than a dog.

That understanding for dogs doesn't help the cat much outside, or in the wild when it bumps into some dog that either doesn't know any cats, or has indeed been conditioned to go after them. Sooner or later every cat that can run around outside has a bad experience with dogs...even if it is only being chased to the tune of howling or barking, a sound which is intolerable for cat ears. In cases of confrontation, very young and old cats react the best, they attack. The sometimes idiotic sounding maxim that the best defense is to attack certainly applies here. Leyhausen reported that even experienced cat-killer dogs shrink back from an attacking cat. Dogs don't want any prey that protects itself by hissing and spitting as well as slicing with sharp claws.

If the cat turns and runs, the dog's hunting reflex is triggered once again. Whatever runs away is prey, that's how the dog was programmed during its evolution, much as the cat was. If the dog catches up (the dog is the better runner over longer distances), any renewed defensive counterattack by the cat will hardly affect the cat-killer dog. Even a moderately sized dog uses its weight to throw the cat down, and once the dog gets its teeth into the cat, the cat is often a goner. The cat can still use its claws to mess up the dog something awful, but in the end the dog will often shake the cat to death, or inflict a fatal bite.

THE REFUGE TREE

It's fortunate that there are trees. A cat always moves along in its territory from refuge tree to tree. The cat succeeds, as a rule, in stopping an attacking dog by an impressive, but sham, counterattack, and because it is faster than the dog over short distances, it can reach the refuge tree and climb up to safety. How (and if) the cat lover gets the cat back down from the top most branches of a tree is another question, the answer to which differs from case to case.

If you get involved in a dog versus cat fight, the best is to provide the cat with a way out. A good weapon is cold water, if available. Also, most dogs give way to a loudly screaming, arm waving human being (although some guard dogs are trained to go after arms and weapons). In some cases, you can toss a piece of wood to divert a dog. The use of any more violent means are certainly not appropriate, of course, for an animal lover.

Violence would be best practiced upon the dog's owner, who is often nearby and who not only doesn't stop his dog from chasing cats but indeed even encourages the dog to do so! It would be well to have a serious chat with a dog owner like that, particularly if he walks his dog often near your cat's territory. Such a dog owner must be made aware of his financial responsibility for any damage caused by his dog; it won't hurt, either, to insure your cat, or have it appraised, even if it doesn't have a pedigree. Most people are more sensitive in their purses than in their consciences.

Luckily, there are horror stories among dog owners about aggressive cats that go for a dog's face and inflict serious eye injuries. This, fortunately, causes many dog owners to put a leash on their dog the moment a cat shows up. Many cats therefore owe their lives to those few magnificent cats that as a rule launch into every dog. We once had such a neighborhood warrior who weighed in at a proud twenty-two pounds. Whenever he sat in the middle of the lawn, the neighbors' dogs fled, tails between their legs, out of the garden.

For these reasons above, a dog isn't a welcomed guest in a cat household. Likewise, it's inappropriate to take a cat to visit a dog household. With care, of course, you could keep the two apart and prevent noisy encounters, but that would really be nerve-wracking for man and pets alike. Unfortunately, this approach often applies just as well to dogs and cats that know each other or perhaps have grown up together. We've seen how a young Shepherd with whom Mao had gotten along just fine on previous visits growled threateningly and chased our cats during a recent visit to our home. The cats didn't show up again until late the next night. Even then, they peered cautiously into all corners to make sure that this dog wasn't still hiding somewhere. You can spare animals this harassment by leaving your dog home when you visit a cat household, and perhaps even pay a cat sitter when we are invited to a dog household.

ENEMIES OF A KIND

The same precaution applies to any visit involving cat strangers. The attempt to get adult cats used to one another should only be made if absolutely necessary. We were able to introduce Einstein, whom my son couldn't keep any longer, nicely into our family circle without any great problems with Bagheera and Mowgli, our two incumbent house cats.

The neighbor's tom Duscha, on the other hand, stays aloof as far as Mowgli is concerned, pursues the smaller Einstein with a raging animosity, but displays an almost abnormal friendliness towards Bagheera. When Duscha meets Einstein in the garden, he chases him into the house, or along a stream that flows by the house. Inside the house, however, Einstein takes a challenging stance to block the food bowl, forcing Duscha to take a humiliating detour. Einstein probably feels stronger in his inner territory, or Duscha finally got the message that we people get into the fray whenever our smaller cat is threatened.

One thing is certain: The most frequent and most dangerous enemy of our loose cats as well as the source of many heart pangs and many vet bills, is the other cat...which is an enemy not only territorially but also as a sexual rival. Even the altered tom may retain a residue of sexual jealousy and under some circumstances get itself embroiled in fights.Unaltered toms will sooner or later unhesitatingly settle the question of just who is the sole ruling pasha of a piece of ground. Unfortunately, one fight doesn't completely close the dispute, because the loser keeps trying to take revenge.

Female cats generally leave toms in peace, though the female herself is such a jealously territorial guardian that fights can break out. That's why you've got to orient yourself as to the surrounding feline world when you (and your cats) move into a new neighborhood. You are the new kid on the block. When you present yourself, as a civilized new neighbor, to your neighbors, the conversation can well encompass cats, theirs and yours.

As so often in life, there are the two usual possibilities: (1) There are many cat lovers. That's good...but also not so good, depending. Cat lovers usually have cats who already have territories and may not like our cats to start running around in them. Or (2) There are few cat lovers, or even none. So our cats are immediately in charge of

territories...but it's not certain whether the neighbors agree with their gardens suddenly becoming territories. Problems are built into situations like that. What is sorely needed to defuse such tinderboxes is charm, our own as well as that of our cats.

TERRITORIAL DISPUTES

Out cat(s) must somehow fit into the established pattern (or modify it?). Fights may be in store. Cats go by the maxim: first come, first served (or, really, come first, hunt first!). A huge black tom who studies proudly, stalks and sprawls out around his territory is surely not about to give up any of his piece of turf without a struggle. The cautious cat lover will certainly not let nature run

its course according to the old adage: may the best cat win, but will take pains to watch for signs of the developing territorial fight and keep it well under control. At least one encounter is inevitable. It then sometimes turns out surprisingly well, something like when two cats live together in one home.

There's a dreadful shrieking, both cats stand each other off with threat-posturing, hissing and spitting...but eventually the encounter fizzles out. Both cats hold their ground, glaring at each other until the nerves of one weaken. At that point, the weaker one moves very, very slowly, without turning its back, and leaves the battlefield. These neighboring cats may now

Cat fights are the cause of most of the injuries a cat brings home. What may start as play can easily escalate to bite and claw wounds. Wounds like this must usually be treated by a vet.

simply avoid any future run-ins, or they may become partners, or even develop a friendship. None of this can be predicted. Sometimes, however, when a cat fight does erupt, it's good for us to break it up. Such a duel is quite a dramatic sight to behold. The only reason that some perverse manager hasn't tried to market such spectacles, like they do cockfights and dog fights, is that cats think only of disappearing the moment any audience shows up...even if they have to scale walls to do it.

A serious fight is in the offing when both cats face each other and make threat postures broadside, hair standing on end, bent tail, and that shriek that melts stone and can infuriate human beings, according to the German poet Scheffel. They strut stiff legged until one decides to attack and leaps at the other. The attacked cat throws itself on its back to get full use of its teeth and all four sets of claws. The attacker, too, does the same to gain the same advantage in weaponry, and both cats tangle together in one spinning ball of clawing, biting and howling like a thousand demons.

And there we have the classic fight in which serious injury is intended and often inflicted. Veteran gladiators among cats are proclaimed by their wounds, shredded ears, deep facial scars, bald spots in the coat, and even lameness due to a mauled paw. Since you don't want all that for your cuddly pussycat, I suggest you intervene on time. In the very first squabble over territory, your cat will be at a disadvantage because an incumbent cat is more determined psychologically. This is the time for your humane water gun.

The native will retreat and your home player will have a chance to escape. Sometimes, on the other hand, yours will suddenly get courageous and pursue the foe a few steps the moment he retreats. That's good for your cat's self-esteem, but you needn't worry about his unfair counterattack upon the retreating cat; the further he gets from you, the more anxious he'll become to get back under your protection.

If you can manage to intervene several times like this, then there's a good chance for a truce of sorts, whereby the cats limit their hostility to verbal insults when their paths cross, or they might just stay out of each other's way completely.Territory-marking cats are very reasonable creatures. They have no wish to get into dangerous fights. Sex is, however, an exception, they fight over that...but so do many other creatures, too. A lot of cat traffic can crisscross a territory, so the owner of the turf marks it with messages. One route of communication is to scratch on trees or posts, with a message like: Here resides a tom cat that's so big you really don't want to mess with him. Another way to send a message is to spray urine. Toms, even altered ones, do it more often than females. Perhaps that's because males are more often involved in belligerent activities.

These spray markings are mainly used to define the limits of the territory, but also the paths the owner usually takes through his territory. Places where the paths of two cats meet are especially informative. Scientists have learned that cats can tell at those intersections (1) who else sprayed there, (2) whether the other sprayer is known, and whether they already had a dispute together before, and (3) whether the other cat always spray here at the same time. Based upon these facts, most cats plan a schedule of patrols through the territory, and try to avoid any confrontation with territory rivals.

Leyhausen and the well-known cat specialist Rosemarie Wolff both reported that cats of a neighborhood often gather together at night for a little friendly socializing, especially toms when they're not in rut and when no females are in heat anywhere nearby. The report goes on to say these cats sit in a circle and only make a barely audible hiss from time to time if any of the cats fails to show proper respect for the intimate atmosphere. All those gathered apparently enjoy this sociable togetherness.

For years I lost sleep by climbing garden and yard fences at the risk of being filled with buckshot by homeowners who thought that I was a burglar. If I ever saw anything, it was fighting and hot pursuits in which my own cats were involved. Then, finally, in my own garden, I witnessed what I had never doubted was true, the scene described by the two cat experts–Leyhausen and Wolff.

One night as I went out to gather in my cats, I saw my three along with the neighbor's tom and two unknown cats sitting at intervals of about six feet from one another under the bushes and trees. I didn't hear any belligerent sounds, and it all seemed quite peaceful. The two unknown cats, however, scooted off when I appeared, and I almost feel bad that I messed up their evening entertainment. Leyhausen was doubtful that any pugnacious tomcat could become an absolute despot of a place. Based upon my own experience and various reports, I beg to differ. In our neighborhood we had a huge tom, presumably with some wildcat blood in him, who tyrannized the other cats. He attacked whenever he saw another feline. Sometimes he lay in ambush for my cats and once rather seriously injured my Siamese Mao.

He was a magnificent, unmistakable creature. I once spotted him about 2 miles from my home. He was apparently patrolling his

Some dog owners condition their dogs to go after cats. A cat doesn't have a chance if it can't find a tree or something to climb up.

superterritory and regularly raiding the territories of other cats to look for trouble. That didn't stop him from taking the opportunity of coming out of the bushes and rubbing affectionately against my legs. Considering that this cat weighed about twenty- five pounds, his affection almost literally threw me off my feet. He let me pet him, but I had to watch out for his claws once his interest and affection ran out.

Leyhausen reports, in contrast to what was cited earlier, the existence of an assassin cat, a serial cat killer in a certain area, that was captured and brought to Leyhausen's institute, where tests showed definitely that this tomcat was an inveterate anticat creature. In his relationship with human beings, on the other hand, this assassin placed enough value to be an affectionate and cuddly pussycat. Leyhausen considered him an exception. I think there are

more of his ilk, and they are doubtlessly responsible for some mysterious disappearances of cats.

If you note any increase in fights on your own grounds (that is, those of your cat) involving a strong, unknown cat, then it's advisable to withdraw your own cat(s) from the combat zone for awhile, despite how hard that decision may be. The cat stranger might then get bored after awhile, lose his taste for your overly peaceful turf and move back to his own territory again. At least you can hope he does. It's best, of course, to live like me, with peaceable cats, whose nature (or perhaps bitter experience) led them to abhor fighting. When other cats visit, my own cats let out a scream to high heaven and scamper off to hide. I interfere only when a cat is cornered. My tom Mao saves himself in situations like that by elegantly leaping up over the bully's head and making straight for the cat door.

A few bursts of my water gun usually wise up strangers. I'm convinced that my water tactics help not only my own cats but also all neighborhood cats, as well as their owners. The number of injuries from cat fights is thus sharply reduced, saving all of us a lot of problems.

It's all in fun. The two cats are on the best of terms with the huge dog. Most likely they grew up together as young animals.

Living with Cats

In this chapter I will discuss a number of unrelated subjects that, collectively, form part of living with a cat.

NEIGHBORS AND BIRD LOVERS

One of the realities of living with a cat is that you must take into account the views and attitudes of other people who may affect the life of your feline friends. These only become important if your cat is an inside—outside feline. However, as you can never be sure your inside only cat will not one day manage to escape your home, these people cannot be discounted. We have already mentioned in a previous

A refuge tree may also be dangerous for a cat. A panic-stricken cat climbs out beyond its normally safe limits and can't get back down. The fire department may be helpful.

chapter the dog owners who masquerade as animal lovers then encourage their pets to chase and attack cats. These rarely understand attempts to reason with them, so they are best dealt with by warning them that you will take legal action against them in the event their dog should attack your cat and either kill it or cause veterinary attention to be needed. Point out to them that you will be seeking not only full compensation for your own loss, but a court order for them to keep their dog under proper control, which they are obliged to do in all western countries, at the least. Failure to comply with such a court order can result in both a fine and the confiscation, and possibly destruction, of their dog. In the event that their dog enters your property to chase your cat, you can further point out that you are within the law to take whatever physical means you care to in defense of said property and your pets living on it. If a dog is on a lead, as is required in order to be under proper control, it cannot attack your cat.

You can often have a meeting of the minds with reasonable hunters in whose hunting area you live. Against the unreasonable ones who shoot cats even in the safe or protected zones you can again point out that you will sue for full compensation. Further, if you are able to obtain their name and address you can advise them you will notify gun associations of their name, and that you abhor the type of people who they allow into their association.

For example, members of the NRA in the USA are under a great deal of pressure from anti-gun people who want gun control legislation. If hunters should shoot a pet, this is a guaranteed magazine headline and another nail in the coffin for gun owners, as well as very poor PR for hunters in general, many of whom are NRA members. Fortunately, hunters in the USA are not normally disposed to shooting at cats, or any other pets, they are more responsible—it is the amateur air gun enthusiasts who are the most likely to do this. Nonetheless, there are morons in all activities and these are no more liked by their fellow hunters than they are by you or me. If you can identify these people report them to the NRA. They have enough on their plates without having gun happy idiots in their midst!

Defense against these is via threats of your suing them. Whenever you spot them, call the police and be prepared to go to court if necessary. Shooting within residential areas is prohibited in all civilized countries. Bird lovers are usually gentle people, and their dislike of cats is more a fear of them. These people usually limit themselves to a hissing or making sounds to shoo the cat away. Others, in their fear for the lives of their feathered friends, burst into a rage and reach for stones or other hard objects. These kinds of people are often helped by a gentle soul massage. If you make them aware that you too are a bird lover, and try your best to prevent your pet dining on the birds they will be more sympathetic to your situation. Often, they regard cat owners as being the sort of people that you dislike in dog owners! Point out the credits of cats in their important role as rodent catchers.

Cats are skilled climbers but may often overdo themselves. They survive falls from great heights, often only with fractures and bruises.

HOW TO BEFRIEND CHILDREN

Yet another group of potential cat haters should be converted into friends: the neighbor's kids. Some think it is fun to chase a cat and see how it scurries up a tree, or try out the new slingshots or play panther hunter with bow and arrow. But there's no sense in being a child-hater. The best recourse is to take any particularly obnoxious little boy into your confidence and present a low key lecture on cats. Kids are thankful when an adult treats them like reasonable grown-ups. Give the kids some candy at appropriate times to keep their association with cats pleasant. So, with the imparting of some feline facts, you can make friends for your cats and help create future cat lovers. Because of my fundamental skepticism about human nature, I sort of back up any success with the kids by assigning them guard duties reinforced by regular allotment of tribute paid in various forms. Children can be astonishingly sharp observers. When I talk with them, I learn a great deal about the territorial behavior of my cats...and also the attitudes of my neighbors! My little associates are invaluable in the search for cats that disappear. You only have to refer to them as 007 or Kojak for them to get right on the case.

DISAPPEARANCES

Luckily, most cats, even those allowed to roam outside, keep to a rather tight schedule. You can count on seeing them show up at definite times. If they're delayed for hours, you can get real upset and worried, and some people even start combing the streets at this point, or checking the neighbors' yards (if you're on good terms with them...which is very advisable). You shine your flashlight under bushes and up into trees and generally make yourself look ridiculous to any passers-by as you whisper your cat's name. In short, you're worried.

Each of my cats was lost all night at one time or another, and Mao was lost for two nights. We went through hell, and apparently the cats did, too. Now they come in late only sometimes, and usually for good reason...like bringing home a mouse or rat. Any reasonable person will understand that a cat lying in ambush for prey is not concerned with the clock or the sensitivities of its human companion.

One day, your cat might actually disappear. Panic is counterproductive; you can do many things. First, call animal shelters in your section of town and give a detailed description of the missing cat. Now is the time it pays to have invested in tattooing your cat's ear; vets can do that with a letter and number code which is then reported to a central pet registry. Anyone can inquire there for the name of the owner of the tattooed cat you find (or who finds you). The question is whether the finder really wants to locate the owner and return the new found and very desirable pussycat. Many families would rejoice if a new cat stepped into their lives, perhaps because they just lost their own beloved cat. Today, the attitude towards keeping what belongs to others is lax, and such people push aside any pangs of conscience about the unknown loser's pain.

If these first efforts are not successful, you can check your municipality's department that deals with the removal of animal bodies (animal control, sanitation, or other department your city may have); some places have animal carcass removal services that are well managed, including detailed records of what animal was run over or otherwise found dead. At least you will learn, for example, that no black cat has been killed in the last few days, which is some consolation for the moment.

Pet shops, news agents and veterinary clinics often let pet owners in their area place missing animal notices in their windows. Local radio stations may also have a lost pets bulletin service at no cost. This can be really beneficial. Don't overlook interviewing your neighbors about whether they saw anything unusual going on the day your cat disappeared. This is the time, too, to press your kiddie (and kitty!) observer corps into service...with the offer of a reward, of course.

Don't forget the societies for the prevention of cruelty to animals (the S.P.C.A. itself and other animal organizations). There are also local initiative groups of animal lovers who keep records of missing animals, and even of suspicious animal dealers. Under some circumstances we should drop in on one of those people. They might even try to sell us back our own beloved cat, all of whose traits and markings we recognize at a glance, but that would be a rare lucky break.

ROAMERS AND VAGABONDS

Don't despair even if success has eluded you for some time. You might be missing your cat for weeks until one day it's suddenly home again in more or less good condition. If that happens to you, I'd say you're the owner of either a cat that genuinely got itself lost, or one that is a rare kind of cat, a roamer. They simply don't stay put in one place. Such cats show up especially in rural areas. These roamers seem to have an inborn tendency to go on 'walkabouts'.

They need you and your home as a base of operations, but they allow themselves the liberty of living elsewhere for weeks. They usually come upon people who suspect they've found a roamer or who accept it as such. I distinguish between roamer and a vagabond. The roamer still has a feeling of where it really belongs, and indeed spends most of its time there. The vagabond, however, is really homeless. It may have been turned loose, or been born of a half-wild female cat that raised it somewhere out in the wild, but then shooed it off. Or it was once part of a large cat group, say on a farm, but for some reason became a loner.

The homeless cat certainly doesn't enjoy its freedom, or at least not always. Such a cat usually makes a desperate search for a new home, and once one is found, is from that moment on no longer a vagabond. An office friend of ours took in an anxious, wandering cat like that. It had such a fear of having to be free again that it stayed away from open doors and windows.

Even an inveterate vagabond, however, knows how to appreciate the amenities of a human household, at least now and then. It's difficult for a sensitive human being not to be adopted by a vagabond cat. You can make it easier on yourself by accepting the vagabond as a vagabond, a sort of part-time cat. Consider it like you do some of your unpredictable friends; that is, be happy to see it if it's there, but don't worry about it if it doesn't come.

There are two probabilities when dealing with vagabonds: (1) It simply fails to return ever again. Either it found a better home elsewhere or, what is more likely, has finally wandered on up into catdom's happy hunting grounds. Or (2) the vagabond gets older and more

comfortable, his visits to you get longer and longer until he's become a house cat.... yours. Only rarely does a cat you've had since kittenhood develop into a vagabond. Cats sometimes decide to leave and seek their fortune elsewhere. I know of a case which involves what we can easily call a zoo. One cat lived on a large piece of property along with three horses, two foals, three dogs, a few goats, some poultry and four other cats. They all got along well together, even the dogs and cats. One little tomcat, however, found it too much for him, and realized he wasn't getting enough petting, either. So he looked five houses further and found a new family that gladly adopted him, with the blessings of his former owner, too. That cat is now a happy 'only' feline.

In another case, a tomcat left his five-cat household and moved in with a farmer who lived in a village (instead of out on the farm). Now, whenever the cat's former lady owner comes into the village to shop, he'll say hello to her, but he won't go back home with her. Different cats have different needs. These two loners found that their former abodes did not satisfy those needs. A cat goes after what it needs.

THE UNCLEAN CAT

Cats that may be unclean at home will fall into one of two types. There is the sprayer, a male that deposits his hardly fragrant scent

anywhere or everywhere, and there is the cat that attends its bowel movements in much the same locations— anywhere. The owners of cats like these are often silent about the problems, but you can smell the problem the instant you set foot in their homes.There may be several reasons for an unclean cat. Sometimes castrations are not done well, and the tom continues to produce so much male hormone that he can still spray like an uncastrated cat. The vet can clear this up by another operation or by shots. Urinary tract disorders or weak sphincter musculature, too, may be the cause (We're not concerned about minor and transient poops— accidents like when a kitten forgets itself while playing.)

Claw-sharpening is a basic need of cats. Good, when the clawing is on a tree stump in the garden. Not so good, when it's on a finely upholstered easychair in the living room.

Continued uncleanliness without apparent physical cause is usually due to psychological reasons. All cats spray to mark their territories. The cat feels so secure in territory number one, its own home, that it doesn't feel the need to spray-mark it. If your cat, however, does start to do this you should ask yourself a few questions:

(1) Has another cat recently visited your home? Or left spray-markings there? If so, your cat is acting out of pure self defense, and you'll have to consider how to prevent such invasion of privacy by the other cat. If necessary, perhaps sealing off from the outside world for a day or two will do it.

(2) Has something recently been changed in your home? Do you have a new family member, a new spouse, or a new boarder whom your cat may feel threatened by? If so, then getting to know the new person better usually resolves the problem.

(3) Were any tradespeople or repairmen working in your home for prolonged periods?

(4) Did your cat have to do battle with another cat outside? After he lost a fight with another tom cat, our Mao relieved himself against the doorpost of the small room in which he alone usually slept.

A cat can also stupidly consider a new piece of furniture reduces or even threatens its territory. You can only hope for a speedy processing or impregnation of that furniture (especially if it includes leather) with your cat's scent, and thereby get it over with before any guests come around.

There are psychologists who offer to analyze your cat's behavior and then advise you of remedies. At the risk of starving out these high cost professionals, please realize that what they really analyze is you, and you can do that to yourself just as well. Those psychologists won't learn anything from talking with your cat. They'll talk with you instead. We have to realize that cats don't behave uncleanly because they're nasty or bad but because some change or event made it appear to them that it was necessary to spray.

Many changes cannot be avoided or undone. What can be done? There are anti-spray products that you apply to the appropriate spots. According to my experience, I can only say that these products provide moderate results. Of course, you can keep on spraying every so often. In that case, I couldn't stand living in the same room because the products nauseate me. The best defense is to give the urinator a fright. Watch him closely until he assumes the very characteristic position that tells you what's going to happen. To urinate, he squats down; but to spray he stands stiff-legged, holds his flicking tail up and does it. His intent is quite unequivocal if he takes this position with his hindquarters against a wall or piece of furniture. You can either yell your loudest No! or, again, resort to your trusty water pistol. The cat must be made to understand that the disadvantages of spraying far outweigh the advantages of territorial security. That often does the trick. A weak solution of ammonium chloride or of household ammonia might help deodorize the spray-marked spots.

In the case of the unclean urinator or defecator, the problem has a different cause. The most common is that the litter tray has not been cleaned enough, so the cat chooses an alternative spot. Once this has happened the scent attracts the cat to use the same spot or one nearby. You must understand that scent from urine does not mark just the spot used but travels into the carpet for quite a distance. It also marks furniture so that simply cleaning the spot may remove the scent in your nostrils, but the cat's sense of smell is infinitely better, so it continues to use the same spot or one near to it. The answer is firstly to try and shut off that part of the room, or the room itself, from the cat while it is retrained. You must ensure the tray is cleaned daily, and it is wise to have two trays at strategic locations. If the room cannot be isolated from the cat you should place one tray where the cat has been fouling, and one where you want it to attend its needs. Now you must watch out and catch the cat in the act if it is not using the tray. Don't yell at it but simply lift it up and place it into the nearest tray and lavish praise on it. Sometimes you can retrain it quickly (as in days), sometimes much patience is needed (as in weeks), but *all* cats can be retrained if your patience holds out. Once it is using the tray you then move this by increments towards the spot you want. No cat is born dirty; it becomes that way through lack of training or lack of cleanliness with respect to its litter tray. Never try to train by rubbing the cat's nose in its own excrement because the cat simply will not understand what you are doing and you just may compound the problem by making the cat coprophagic.That means a fecal-eating cat! When you have rubbed the cat's nose into fecal matter it has no choice but to lick this off. If this idiotic old fashioned idea is repeated the cat may actually become accustomed to the taste as strange as this may seem. Bear in mind that humans living in the filth of ghettos do get used to it, which sounds equally as strange. That is the comparison.

THE INFIRM CAT

There are blind cats and deaf ones, too, whose other senses permit them to easily come to grips with life and their surroundings. Such cats, of course, can't be allowed to roam around freely outside; however, they can still live a happy, quality life inside the house, and perhaps also in securely closed off yards and gardens. Vets have assured me that a cat who has lost a leg learns very quickly to deal with it, even to the point of still being able to jump.

But what's to be done for a fifteen-year-old cat who undergoes surgery twice in one year for removal of tumors, and then develops a third one? Or is the cat's life still happy enough after a traffic accident that leaves the cat to drag itself through the house with two crippled forelegs and a grotesquely deformed spine? I know of cases like both of these.

Modern veterinary medicine allows us to operate on all internal organs and keep cats alive even under unfavorable circumstances. So, in these cases where almost everything can be saved, the question is whether the cat will find its life still worth living...and only the cat's interest counts in this decision, not the owner's selfish desire to keep his beloved animal just as long as humanly possible. A decision like this, with a cat, is set within narrower limits than it would be for a human being, who, of course, can still enjoy a great intellectual and spiritual life even in a wheelchair. A cat lives physically, and when its body and physical powers are lost because of severe damage, it's

not a decent cat's life anymore: it should be ended. The decision to terminate the cat's life will be determined by the quality of life the cat can still enjoy. If you are uncertain and your vet knows your cat from having treated it over any span of time, you should weigh his or her advice highly.

YOUR CAT: A VACATION MILLSTONE?

I know a great many people who would like to have cats. But they don't want to risk it. They will say: Sure, I like cats, but I also like to travel, twice, three times a year, sometimes a long weekend. So what do you do with a cat? There is merit in this thought, and cat lovers certainly worry about these things. Yet I don't think it is grounds enough for doing without the company of a cat. Where there's a will, there's a way. There are just as many possibilities to take a cat on vacation as there are to take a baby.

Conditions are sometimes optimal. A couple I know just enjoyed a four-month creative working vacation in a country house...with their magnificent Siamese tomcat. The cat had a great time, too. The country house stood alone, almost five miles to the closest village. There was no cat competition anywhere around. The cat patrolled around the house, cleaned up the available mice, and never strayed more than about fifty yards from the home. That amount of territory apparently satisfied him for his home away from home. The couple had no trouble whatsoever getting him back into the house whenever they wanted, especially at night. That's how to have a relaxed vacation with a cat. On the other hand, if your holiday is planned to be in a hotel, or in a number of these while touring then it is a bad idea to take the cat . . . It will certainly not enjoy it, and there will always be the risk it may escape if the cleaning maid opens the door while it is free in the room. Once out, you'll have a difficult time looking for a cat (a strange place often includes large, unknown buildings, large gardens or fields, or perhaps treacherously busy traffic just outside the door). Frankly, I wouldn't have a relaxing vacation under those conditions.

Short weekends from Saturday morning to Sunday evening are less of a problem for adult cats, who can be left home alone. If a neighbor or friend looks in Sunday morning to check on food and the cat toilet, and to give a few ounces of tender loving care, so much the better. Otherwise, a generous portion of food and water suffices until your return. However, I wouldn't leave a very young kitten, or one new to the household, alone like that; you would have to forego weekend trips for a time.

If you are one of the many people who vacation in a trailer or motorhome you should be able to take your cat without too much problem. This becomes their home away from home and they do get familiar with it if you are a regular RVer (recreational vehicle traveler). Kelsey-Wood, some of whose cats are seasoned travelers, both internationally, and via motorhome, gives the following advice. 'Some cats are definitely better travelers than others, but all will get

Organized groups of thieves are often behind cat disappearances. A tattoo in the cat's ear is some protection. Laboratories have agreed not to buy any tattooed cats.

used to regular traveling if they are very much loved family cats, rather than simply cats living in a home with you. Some can be let out for a walk at every overnight stop; others you must watch constantly. Some owners have trained their cats to accept the restriction of a long leash when outside of their trailer. The most worrying trips are the first two or three when you find out which sort of cat you have—one that panics and runs away a short distance, or one that takes a very cautious approach and works outwards after carefully scent marking the wheels of your trailer. When you stop overnight, pick a quiet campground well away from the road, and choose a quiet site, if possible. If the cat is new to RVing do not let it out on one-night stops, but wait until you will have two or more nights in the same location. Let it out on the second night, by which time you will know if there are dogs or other things that might frighten it. I say night because we have found that cats are more at ease under darkness. There is less noise and disturbances to make them edgy. They feel more confident of being able to move around without being seen. You should stay with them unless you know they are totally reliable, as a couple of ours have become. However, if you are not a very regular RVer, as in full time or almost every weekend, it is always better to leave the cats at home—they will be happier, and you will worry a lot less. Were it not for circumstances, we would never have taken ours. We are thankful only one was ever permanently lost over the many thousands of miles we traveled with them. But we did satisfy ourselves that cats can indeed make veteran travelers and met hundreds of vacationers who always take their cat(s) with them.'

BOARDING A CAT

An alternative to taking pussycat with you on holiday is to leave it in a boarding cattery. Prices are not so high that you can't cost this as part of your several weeks of vacation. Unfortunately, many boarding homes keep cats in single cages. Only the more expensive cat 'hotels' offer more space, even with a small enclosed aviary type outdoor facility attached to their cage. Human contact is sometimes lacking. A well-known vet told me that every cat who suffers this experience develops a more or less serious neurosis. The neurosis usually clears up afterwards, back home in the accustomed surroundings. But there's no guarantee.

Cats often pick up diseases in such places, even if they're kept alone and don't mix with the other cats. Veterinarians attribute this susceptibility to a certain loss of immunity or lowered resistance associated with being left along. You must select a cattery with diligence. Choose one where there are solid partitions between each cage as this will dramatically reduce the risk of direct or proximinal spread of disease. Of course, your cat must be up to date with all of its vaccinations—this is often obligatory with the cattery. If it is not, look for another boarding feline hotel.

CAT SITTERS

The best place for your cat is to stay at home in its accustomed surroundings,

and be fed and watered there. That's easily done with a little thought and planning. The ideal is for a close relative or friend to move in while you're gone. Considering the crime rate today, many vacationers place a guard in their homes. A house pet can be included in the guard's duties, and the security organization will assign a guard who gets along well with cats.

Finally, there is an increasing number of cat sitter organizations that operate on the basis of mutuality. That is, your vacation will be covered by a sitter for your cats, and you obligate yourself to cover someone else at another time. Permanent relationships are often found this way, so the same sitters care for the same cats for future vacations. Since cats are known to be animals of habit, such an arrangement could be advantageous.

I don't recommend trying to keep your own cat(s) plus the one(s) you're sitting, in the same home. That might appear to be quite a convenient arrangement, but it usually turns out bad. It's better to commute once or twice a day between the two cat households. That avoids constant concern over inter-cat affairs. There are also professional 'sitter' companies and individuals. In the latter case do check out their credentials because you would not want to come home to a house devoid of its furniture and maybe even the cat!

Danger lurks even in the neighbor's yard. The snail poison with which the neighbor protects his lettuce patch is also poisonous for cats.

An expressive cat countenance. The wide-open eyes and cupped ears indicate a lot of interest. The tilted head expresses trust and an urge to play.

MOVING TO A NEW HOME

Should you move, always take your cat with you rather than sending it with the furniture van as luggage in its cat box. When you arrive at the new house give your cat a drink and a favored treat dinner. Keep it in the home until it has inspected all rooms, and you have unpacked some familiar furniture which will carry its scent. Although some cat owners suggest keeping the cat indoors for one, or even two days, this is not really necessary. Much depends on the individuality of the cat, and is not even related to its age. Your cat will decide itself whether or not the new home is to its liking, and keeping it in beyond a few hours will not persuade it to stay if it doesn't like the house. This will be based on whether the home has an appealing scent to it (maybe it had dogs or cats in it before), and if the rooms and views are appealing. The garden will be very important. If this has plenty of trees, shrubs, and interesting hiding places this will appeal more than if it is open. Likewise, if it came from a nice home and garden the cat is unlikely to enthuse over an apartment or similar place that is a backward step to pussy, if not to your family. If the new home is more or less on par with the old one, then the crunch decision will be how attached it is to its owners. Do remember never to compare dogs with cats over house moves. A dog is a pack animal. Wherever the pack is, that is home—and you and your family are the pack to a dog. A cat is very territorially minded, so a change is much more traumatic to it. Take heart, however, for while cats are famed for long treks back to a former home, these are very much the exception rather than the rule. It is a case that when they happen they often make headline news—the millions of cats that annually move homes without problem are hardly news items.

Cat Communications

All human beings who have cats speak with them... preferably, of course, when they are alone together. The sweet nothings you tell each other are not for other human ears, and most certainly not for non-cat-lovers. Otherwise you could soon acquire a reputation for being somewhat odd. Your cat seems to have a fine feel for whether you're just babbling along to make conversation or whether you really want to tell it something. We've already seen that cats understand recurrent instructions, announcements and orders, like No, Dinner, Here I am, and Want to go out? You also have to admit that a cat has a fine sense for recurrent movements, body positions and vocal tones, all of which are also used as clues to what's going on. My cats come running from all corners of house and yard when I say Come on, we're going down into the cellar, or Come on out into the yard with me; the cats come even before I've put my hand on the doorknob. Cellar is their greatest pleasure because they're not otherwise allowed down there, where they love to climb over all the shelving and explore all the splendid little hideaways and niches. I have fun demonstrating to the skeptics among my

friends and acquaintances how my cats seem to understand every word.

HOW YOUR CAT TALKS TO YOU

It amazes people when you can tell them what your cat wants and what it will do in a moment. Since a cat's range of reactions is rather narrow, that prediction feat is not all that difficult to stage for non believers. Here is a selection of things a cat expresses:

I feel good.
I don't feel well.
I'm in a friendly mood.
Leave me alone!
I want to go out.
I'm hungry.
I'm afraid.
I want to play.
I've got something interesting to watch.
I'm headed somewhere to do my duties.

Siamese. Members of this breed are svelte and lithe in appearance.

I'm bored.

The cat has mimicry, body language, tail signals and voice to express itself. The use of these means, however, varies from breed to breed, and from individual to individual. There are meow-talkative and meow-taciturn cats. There are pantomimists who almost spell it out for you and those who play guess my line with you until you decipher their subtle hints.

The change in a cat's facial expressions is one of the most unambiguous mood indicators. A cat's smooth face, wide open eyes, alert and forward directed ears can't be misunderstood...that all means peaceful but watchful. The first sign of unrest or anger is a neutral (but not really blank) look. The eyes slowly narrow, the ears bend sideways, wrinkles now crease the face, and the lips rise (or retract) slowly. In certain cases all that turns into the pronounced defensive attitude, with horizontally held ears, grimacing face, bared fangs and a hiss that sounds like an angry venomous snake. Whoever doesn't understand these signals and approaches a cat like that shouldn't wonder why they're scratched or even bitten.

BODY LANGUAGE

This expressive facial language is matched by body language. A peaceful, tranquil cat often sits back on its haunches, with its forepaws evenly together in front, and its tail neatly wrapped around towards the front. In this position, a cat is calm and can be spoken to, and can be inspired very quickly to play or join in other activities.

Your cat enjoys another restful position to achieve relaxation and detachment: It stretches out on one side, all four legs extended. It feels good, and wants to slowly fall off to sleep. That's the sleep position of cats that feel completely at ease and safe in their home. Sometimes the cat will bend its head into a sharp angle to its body. It's especially cute when both forepaws are drawn up over the eyes to screen them from daylight or lamplight.

The next maneuver is similar looking, except that the cat rolls in front of you for another purpose. Einstein first rubs his head on my feet, then throws himself into a perfect somersault until he lays out straight as an extended cat. The purpose is quite simple, he wants his belly scratched. In general, this sprawling out on the back is a cat's defensive position, and it shows a great trust when the cat acts this way towards its human companions, to whom it is using this language in a context of affection, not as combat tactics. This position is not one of humility, as it is with dogs.

Many cats cannot suppress their defensive reflex completely or at all in this position, so they make scratching movements with the back legs. Some caution is advisable because the more a cat gets used to being petted this way, the more this defensive reflex disappears, and that could make your cat more of a pushover in any cat fights.

What I call the bunker position is one of watchfulness, unrest, even fear. The cat is, so to say, reduced to just the bulk of its body–forepaws under the chest, the tail close to or under the belly. The head is held low. This is the position taken when the arrival of an unknown cat is anticipated, especially when the waiting cat is on high ground. From this bunker position, the forepaws can be deployed lightning fast to keep the opponent at bay.

If the bunker fails, the cat then goes into the tank position, a more aggressive threat stance characterized by a highly arched back, a humpback, and presented broadside to the opponent. The rear part of the tail is spread horizontally a short distance away from the body, and the forward part bent downwards. This posture enlarges the cat's silhouette, making it a more imposing and threatening opponent.

Leyhausen demonstrated that cats orient themselves upon their opponents' silhouettes. This combat orientation, often accompanied by hissing and screeching, is so unequivocal that you can assume another cat appeared as an opponent even though you don't actually see it. My own cats sometimes come in out of the garden and assume one of these body positions behind the cat door. That tells me in no uncertain terms that an unfriendly visitor from next door has come over again.

A cat often presents itself in a particularly friendly way of greeting you. The cat holds its tail up high as it rubs its head and sides against your legs. When you reach down and pet the cat, it presses its hindquarters against your hand. This is both a sexual challenge and an act of submission performed by tomcats as well as females. It's rather common in the animal world for males who feel inferior to act as females as a protection against attacks. If you were on the same animal level as the presenting cat, it would next make a nose and anal check. It would shove its nose into your face, then turn around to offer its own anal area to be sniffed. As a human being, of course, you don't have to do that; it's only a ritual anyway. The rubbing against you means that your cat wants to re-impregnate you with its scent after you've come back from a more or less long absence. When presenting, the cat's tail plays an important role.

THE ELOQUENT TAIL

The cat's tail is more than a mere appendage, and more than only a stabilizer for walking and jumping. A cat with an erect tail is friendly and in the best of moods. My cats always erect their tails whenever I speak with them, the tips describing elegant little curves around in the air. That's often an invitation to pet, play, feed or open a door.

If this tail motion gets more frenzied and the tail is held more horizontally, the cat is getting excited about something, perhaps an unusual noise, a prey animal, a fly, another cat, a dog, or a person. In any case, the cat's attention is fixed on something. If the tail starts to whip, some action is imminent. The cat often crouches down and patters or treads a few times with its feet, then readies itself to jump or to stalk. My cats do that when they see the flutter of a butterfly or bird, but also when they want to playfully ambush one of their cat buddies. The tail is an important indicator here, too, during these playful antics. As long as the flicking tail doesn't thicken, or its hair doesn't stand on end, you can consider the whole thing an enjoyable sporting event between two friendly cats. Once, however, the tail flattens out into a brush, which is particularly impressive in shorthaired cats, look out for a squabble. In that case, it's best to intervene before they start hissing and tearing at each other.

Still another tail message tells you that your cat doesn't have any time for you at the moment. The tail is held almost horizontally, with only the tip pointing somewhat upwards. The cat heads quite purposefully in some direction, and usually doesn't stop for anything. If you speak to it, and the tail goes up momentarily, then the whole thing wasn't so important anyway, and it's ready to respond to its master's voice. If the tail flicks vigorously from its base several times, then it wants something. The cat wants you to follow it and do something, like open a door. This behavior can also be an invitation to play cops and robbers, in which case the cat jumps a few feet away, perhaps hints at a threatening broadside stance, jerks its tail once again and finally tears off through the house. Einstein likes for me to come after him and say Are you playing the big bad bear cat again? and then stumble after him behind chairs or curtains. Then he paws at me, without claws, of course, and repeats the jump-off ritual. When he's played out, he throws himself on his side and waits for me to scratch him.

It's interesting how a cat, so to speak, revs up with its tail just before a big jump. The cat is sitting say in front of a table it wants to jump up on; the tip of its tail jerks nervously. If your best piece of Meissner porcelain is resting quietly on that table, you still have an instant to shout a vigorous No! My Siamese tom Mao would always stop as ordered but would loudly complain to me about it. He would actually scold me.

A cat can in fact scold you. Cat talk is very expressive, significantly more so than barking. Two tones can be identified in cats. One tone appears to be just for human beings, and the other for other cats. Communication among cats is mostly silent, except for sexual and bellicose affairs. I've already mentioned the screeching and catwailing of females in heat and toms in rut, as well as their threatening battle cries. My own cats generally speak among themselves only when they bump into one another and check each other out via a quick sniff, at which time they utter a soft 'gruu.'

Actual meowing is reserved for communicating with us human beings. Here's how I explain that. We are a surrogate mother for domestic cats. Little kittens always call out in tiny mewing laments and cries when they need help, a help they can't expect from any other cats.

MEOWS FOR HUMANS

Some sounds recur and have specific meanings. Most cats have a typical, recognition and greeting sound, which they utter when they suddenly bump into someone in the house, when they come in from outside, or when you visit them in their favorite spot. The sound is monosyllabic and varies in musical tone from cat to cat. At times it sounds like mi, but like mae at other times. Bagheera utters a rapid succession of mis when he wanted to come in from outside. It also means it is time to give him some attention, and also to get some food into his bowl. This recognition call is quite useful if you're looking for your cat outside or even inside. I've gotten my cats to (usually!) answer to my calling out Where are you? That's helpful

when you're trying to find out if you've inadvertently locked your cat(s) in or out. Sometimes they use this call when you're very busy, but your cats think, however, that you'd best dedicate the time to them instead.

Cats utilize a particularly expressive meow when they're sitting by a closed door through which they want to go out or come in. This call, Be kind enough to open up! is tirelessly repeated, each time growing more urgent and longer drawn out, finally turning plaintive. If for some reason your can't immediately comply with this demand, the wailing can drive you up the wall.

A cat employs a similar, long drawn out call to say it's hungry. This call, too, is so unmistakable that you'll soon recognize it. Mao used it incessantly as he raced me (and beat me) to the refrigerator. As he waited for me to catch up, he kept looking over his shoulder...and woe befall me if I stopped somewhere on the way, in which case he'd intensify his wailing. Mao kept right on vocalizing as his meal was being prepared, warmed up or cut up. Comic relief came when I sat his full bowl down under his nose, at which moment his insistent cries died in his throat, and gave way to the happier sounds of chomping and lip-smacking.

Some cats, noting that you have indeed taken the can of food from the pantry and the can opener from the drawer, instantly stop their 'moaning

This kitten is using all of its senses: Eyes are fixed on target, ears localize it by sound, and the tactile whiskers are forward in anticipation of feeling the target object.

or complaining' and start to rub against your legs in anticipation of what flavor they're getting—others simply keep up the moaning until the bowl reaches the floor!

Almost all of my cats also used to let out a plaintive meow somewhere in the house. When we then reacted by calling out Where are you? What are you up to? Come! they suddenly appeared, visibly happy to see us. This call they sent out to us from somewhere in the house is quite clearly the call of a small, lonesome kitten who is calling to its mother. An adult cat may not have heard from or seen the rest of the family for awhile, and now it's just waking up from a nap and wants to find out who else is home.

PURRING—A RIDDLE

We still don't know for sure why a cat purrs. The cat clearly makes something vibrate, which you can feel by holding your hand on a purring cat. Whether that's due to bones in the gums or whatever else, is really unimportant for us to know.

Purring is in general an expression of contentment and happiness. If your cat doesn't purr when you stroke it, you should wonder why. Small kittens purr when they suckle at their mother's teats, and the mother purrs, too. Purring may serve to dissipate possible aggressive behavior on both sides. My cats often start to purr even when I just speak to them.

Recent studies show that even seriously ill cats purr. There's no conclusive explanation. A possible one would be that the cat is aware of its desperate condition and is calming itself by means of a sort of auto-suggestion or hypnosis.

Every cat owner will discover and get to recognize yet other sounds and vocalization in his cat(s). It's important, for example, to understand a cat's cry for help, which differs from its battle cry. The call (or scream) for help comes from deep down in the chest, and ends up piercingly shrill. This scream for help is so unmistakable that it would get me to leap up stark naked out of the bathtub!

The Cat's Senses

If you really want to feel respect for your cat, then look at it as a wonder of nature...with abilities of which we human beings can only dream, or which we can imitate only by employing great technical means. Take just the physical prowess: A human being who could jump as high in proportion to his body size or run short distances as fast as a cat would be the Olympic athlete of all time. Whoever could bend or contort his body as well as a cat can would be the rubber man attraction at any circus in the world.

CATS' EYES

The cat's sensory performance is even more astonishing. Its eyes have continued to dumbfound cat

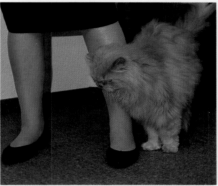

A cat rubs its head on your leg as a greeting for a human friend. The cat also "marks" the leg with some scent to say "You belong to me."

lovers and experts. Most people find them beautiful, witness how novelists give their women characters cat eyes. Their performance is extraordinary. What first becomes obvious is the extreme variability of the cat eye. In bright sunlight the pupil contracts into a narrow, hardly visible slit. In fading light it dilates into a large, dark hole, around which the iris can hardly be recognized. Through this opening the cat takes in any available light. In complete darkness, however, the cat can't see anything. Then it relies on its other senses.

Towards the front, a cat has a somewhat narrow field of vision, which has its reason. When a cat goes outside,

A cat, satisifed with itself, the world and its human companions.

A cat in typical threat stance: The broadside approach with hair standing on end and the "bottle-brush" tail. An imposing figure. We assume that cats orient themselves by the silhouette of the opponent as to whether a fight is advisable or not.

you can see it first takes a sweeping panoramic look, like a submarine commander rotates his periscope. A cat isn't immediately interested in static, that is, immobile objects, but turns its most intense attention only towards whatever moves. That's similar to us in a theater, where we concentrate on what's happening on the stage, but are only vaguely aware of events in the loge or box seats, or other rows near the stage.

Concentration on one target is critical for the cat, a hunting predator. It sees amazingly sharp, especially at a distance between about six and twenty feet, and can estimate distance exceedingly well.

A cat's excellent night vision is possible because a reflective layer of tissue behind the retina redirects the remaining or residual light back again so the cat gets a second image, a reinforcement of the primary image. This reflective layer also reflects more intense light, say from a flashlight or a car's headlights, thus making cat's eyes glow in the dark. The proportion of rods (= rod-shaped cells) to cones (= cone-shaped cells) in the cat's light-sensitive retina is greater than in man. Cats have twenty-five rods to one cone, while man has four rods to one cone, and rods are more sensitive to light than cones.

Cones, on the other hand, are responsible for color vision. We've only discovered those for green and blue in cats, who may indeed be somewhat colorblind. The cat, a nocturnal predator, couldn't care less. This might be the time to recite the old saying: All cats are black at night.

WHISKER TIP RADAR

The cat carries out its night patrols with the confidence and certainty of a somnambulist, thanks also to its highly sensitive whiskers—vibrissae which act like radar. The cat projects an airwave out ahead of itself as it moves along in the dark. If the airwave strikes an object, say a tree trunk, it bounces back and travels via the whiskers to the brain, where it announces the object.

Everyone knows, too, that cats measure off spaces with their whiskers, such as whether they can slip through a narrow passage. We assume that this sensitive organ also picks up a great deal of other information, like the vibrations produced by the movement of other animals.

These whiskers are also matched by other hairs over the eyes that tell the cat about objects looming ahead that could hurt its eyes. They

wink or let their inner eyelid (the nictitating membrane) close down to protect their eyes. Cats also have good tactile (touch) perception in the hairless snout and hairless foot pads. Cats use

This cat language can hardly be misunderstood: Back hunched, tail hairs standing on end, ears laid out, lips retracted, and hissing all add up to "Leave me alone!"

"Am I going to get through here or not?" The kitten's whiskers help it to gauge the width between posts. Similar tactile hairs protect the eyes from injury.

their nose to test the temperature of their food, and will jerk back if it's too hot or cold. A cat's playful pawing of an object tells the cat about that object's size and shape.

HEARING

Ears play an important role in a cat's orientation within its environment. You can see that in the ear is a very large acoustic funnel in proportion to head size in most cat breeds. These ears are provided with a large number of muscles to let the cat turn them to locate sources of sounds. The sounds are then transmitted to the inner ear, a complex system of acoustic passages, the labyrinth, where they are processed for receptors in the brain. This gives the cat three-dimensional hearing which can sort out different sounds and localize them. That means the cat can precisely determine that a beetle is creeping through the grass six feet away, and that a mouse is twitching three feet further than the beetle. We believe that based only on its hearing ability, a cat can jump successfully on that mouse.

SMELL & TASTE

The senses of smell and taste are closely associated in cats, though the sense of smell predominates. We've all seen how a cat sniffs everything, especially, of course, its food. Every human being, too, who comes in contact with the cat is sniffed, and, if necessary, properly perfumed with the

Recognition greeting by nose bumping. The laid-back ears indicate that they aren't yet quite sure whether they know each other.

cat's scent glands (on its head and flanks). Even if the cat is not a nose animal in the same league as the dog, it still has twice as much nasal mucous surface as we do. We can only assume that such a large surface provides the cat with a great deal of information.

In addition, the cat has an accessory organ, Jacobson's organ, named after its discoverer. To use this organ, the cat lifts its lips, opens its mouth a little and draws in the air. This probably helps the cat to test the edibility of food. Cats can turn down spoiled food before tasting it. That organ is also used when the cat checks out the scents of unknown cats or when it examines their rear ends. The cat's sense of taste may not be as developed as its sense of smell. The reason is that its tongue is covered with tiny, horny rasp-like hooks to enable the cat to use it as a tool. The taste receptors are crowded off to the edges of the tongue. The greater number of taste buds on the tongue of a dog would explain why it has a 'sweet

tooth' and the cat, generally, does not. Together, however, smell plus taste both give the cat a powerful taste perception, which is most likely why the cat is often such a finicky, fastidious eater. A great danger in all of this is that ailments that affect the cat's nasal mucous can make it suddenly lose its appetite. What a cat can't smell, it doesn't want to eat.

SUPERSENSORY CATS

The heart of this whole sensory matter is that the cat doesn't apply these extraordinary senses separately, but fully integrated as a whole. This allows the cat to perform extraordinary feats, which have given cats the reputation of possessing a sixth, even a seventh, sense, and of being telepathic and prophetic. All of this throws the poor cat right back into medieval witchery, some of which is getting to be the fad again in some circles today, where devil worship, black masses and black cat sacrifices go on. England also has its ghost cats.

The cat lover has to decisively oppose such involvement of cats in dire events, for our cats can only suffer from it. Most phenomena have natural explanations. The fact that we can't explain everything yet is most likely because we still know too little about cats. We really don't need miraculous and supernatural cat wonders and wonder cats. There are quite enough wondrous cat things to marvel at as it is.

We find it quite wondrous enough, for example, to find our cats waiting for us at the door when we come home. The explanation is most likely that we usually park near the house and the cats sharp hearing can pick up and identify any peculiarities of our motor sounds, or the opening and closing of the car door, and then associate that with us. If not, then certainly it must be our footsteps on the driveway and the tinkling of our keys.

Even if that's not really wondrous or miraculous, it surely indicates intelligence, if we define intelligence as learning ability and as the recognition and organization of recurring events.

Stories of how cats have found their way home are so numerous and so well documented that you can hardly doubt their veracity. The most believable of these stories and reports are the ones that have the cat coming home from a distance not greater than sixty miles, though greater distances are

This cat has assumed a defensive stance, but not aggressively, just anxiously. The position of the tail tells us that this cat will spring away at the first chance it gets.

apparently possible. In this homing ability, too, some see parapsychological, that is, extrasensory or supersensory elements. But here, too, the natural explanation is wondrous enough. Scientists believe that a combination of senses shows the cat the way home. The cat still has in its memory the sun's position as it looks at this, and can calculate the difference in the sun's angle between home and the place where the cat is now lost. Also the cat's sensitive footpads can apparently pick up emanations from the earth's magnetic field.

Moreover, Leyhausen believes that cats acquire a sound image of their immediate home surrounding, which they use for orientation during the last phase of their journey home. A cat, so to say, possesses the navigational instruments of a modern ship or aircraft.

The gift of prophecy, too, is wondrous, but explainable. Just before the devastating earthquake of 1776 struck Messina, Italy, a famous cat, it is said, drove his master out of the house. We know, of course, that many tremors or oscillations can precede an earthquake, but human beings can't feel them all. The cat, however, picks up the unnerving information from its sensitive footpads and highly perceptive sense of balance. Other animals, too, have similar sensory receptors. In the earthquake regions of China, birds, rats and snakes are considered earthquake predictors.

It's no less a wonder how a cat with a fine sense of smell can notice a smoldering fire at home even before its master detects it, and can excitedly make him aware of the danger. It was also a wonder how a cat seized its master's trousers and pulled him toward the door and out of the house just two minutes before a devastating air raid on Magdeburg in 1944. The cat heard the drone of approaching bombers minutes before the listening devices of the FLAK units detected them. Riddles do exist. How about cats that find their masters in places where the cats have never been (or were not known to have been there before)? Perhaps the answer is telepathy, brain waves, which we can't detect but the cat can. Studies have been made

The cat has an excellent sense of touch in its footpads.

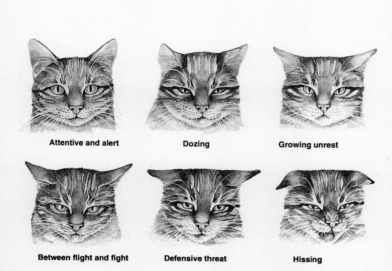

Attentive and alert   Dozing   Growing unrest

Between flight and fight   Defensive threat   Hissing

in which investigators concentrated on causing a cat to act in a definite way, like going to a certain food bowl. Results were not indicative, but were somewhat better than the probability of random occurrence.

Cats are known to have apparently sensed the imminent death of their human companion and cuddled up to him as he lay dying. That's a moving, pathetic image...but possibly explainable by a change in body tone or odor. But do we really want to know all the scientific details? As lay people who love cats, we can rejoice in just experiencing these amazing animals. Rejoice that such an extraordinarily gifted creature (who certainly must view us as some kind of stumblebums or huge inept cats) desires to share our lives with us.

Stories, Famous People & Cats

All that has been written and said about cats would fill a library. I'll just zip quickly through some of the oral and written lore to perhaps whet your appetite. We cat lovers work on a daily basis to create oral lore and a store of usable information. It's really heart warming to learn how many nice people suddenly appear when you reveal yourself to be a cat buff. All of these people speak endearingly of their cats, and you find yourself listening to one cat anecdote after another. Many of these anecdotes are the same, obviously, because the cats are the same, at least in many respects. Many are hand-me-downs from well-known people who said them some time ago. Fact and fiction are often hard to separate, but since I've been dealing with cats, I believe (almost) everything.

There are stories that cover a cat that leaps voluntarily into a swimming pool and paddles around; a cat that opens a cookie tin and steals a cookie; a cat that activates a bell when it wants to be hoisted up out of the garden and back to its home several stories up; the cat that plays with a budgerigar (or parakeet); the cat who calls its huge Newfoundland dog friend for help against other cats.

A favorite kind of story deals with the hunting prowess of cats, who (in German stories) know how to lay out the day's catch in the proper hunter format required before the trumpet or hunting horn can sound over it. Another kind of story tells of the athletic performance (that is, sham combat) of our cats. Since we all abhor violence, we have to embellish somewhat to make our cats' battles sound good. One's own cat is always attacked, never the aggressive attacker, but if so, then only in legitimate defense of its own territory. That's certainly permissible, isn't it? Fighting spirit and tactics of one's own tiger are, at most, mentioned only incidentally. Even the owners of notorious bullies can barely hide their satisfied grins between simulated worry creases when they sanctimoniously warn you: Your cats better not get near my Putzi. He's number one around here!

The cat and dog story is yet another kind. A friend of mine had a tiger cat who lived peaceably with a German Shepherd. One day the cat had four cute little kittens, and the dog joined

wholeheartedly into the new family. As the kittens grew, they were allowed to romp only with their mother and with Uncle Dog. They played catch with him, and the whole household was happy about the nice relationship. A variant of catch one day, however, horrified everyone (the human beings, that is). Uncle Dog was picking up a kitten broadside on his snout, then throwing his head up, sending kitty cat several yards through the air. The kitty fell, as befits a cat, on all fours. Then kitty got in line again with its littermates, who all wanted the same ride. County fair attraction! Roller coaster for small kitty cats. I didn't believe it...I saw it with my own eyes.

FAIRY TALE AND LEGENDARY CATS

A great deal of what has come down to us as cat history is legend. I've covered some of it earlier. Cat (fairy) tales are another means of enlightening us on the role of cats in times long gone. All nations that ever had cats, had cat fairy tales, fables and other stories, but with noteworthy differences.

In Europe, in the Christian occident, we find cats associated with deviltry and

Pure love. This cat ecstatically closes its eyes, rubs with its head and bumps noses, paying its human friend a great compliment... by considering her a nice giant cat.

Although the cat is by nature a predator, it gets along quite well on farms with other animals. This lamb has nothing to fear, which is clearly evident by the lack of this mother ewe's interest in her baby lamb's new friend.

witchcraft. In *The Tale of Someone Who Went Out to Learn Fear*, there's a treasure guarded by two gigantic cats with eyes as large as coffee cups. In *Hansel and Gretel*, the old witch is always shown with her cat. In the *Bremen City Musicians*, a cat has an important clawing role in foiling some robbers.

In the Orient, on the other hand, Indian and Chinese tales emphasize the cat's useful role as mouser and ratter, which is no surprise for these people whose staple food is every kind of cereal grain. The magical element consists of the cat's fantastic success in annihilating these rodents. In many tales, only one cat suffices to clear out a rodent plague from a whole city, and this supercat is often rewarded with the hand of the princess in marriage. We can conclude from this type of story that owning a cat in those days was happiness and privileged.

In 17th century Europe,

these stories became more of an art form by definite authors than merely anonymously transmitted lore. Perrault wrote *Puss in Boots*, a tomcat born in the Age of Enlightenment and who didn't need any magic at all...he was simply clever. His repertoire of tricks and abilities led his master to fame and fortune, including the hand of the king's daughter.

You may well ask how he could so intimidate peasants and servants that they would tell people that their own masters' lands and castles all belonged to the cat. Wasn't that all witchcraft again? Consider first what you would say if you were ever confronted by a speaking pussycat wearing boots, a cat that issued orders to you? Well, there's the answer, a very rational explanation...just the stuff of the Age of Enlightenment.

Puss in Boots made the international rounds. In

Russia, a cat (with the same tricks, but without boots) is the sole inheritance of a certain Ivan, whom the cat leads to fame and fortune. In the English-speaking world, of course, there's Dick Whittington and his cat, and so on. In Germany, the Grimm brothers used this story. Ludwig Tieck wrote a satire on it, until by the 19th century, the literary cat (usually tom cat) story emerged.

THE LITERARY CAT

In his 1908 study on Tomcat Murr and his Tribe, the literary scientist Dr. Franz Leppmann had this to say: A man's animal is his hunting partner, the dog. But as soon as man became devoted to (or encumbered with?) domestic activity, the cat showed up, too. Medieval imagination peopled the black magic laboratories with cats along with the ravens. 'The cat is the sage's companion,' said the alchemist in one of Theodore Storm's stories, and you have to admit that this silent, clever animal is a better companion for the intellectual than are many other four-legged animals.

Leppmann was describing a 19th century phenomenon: cats were becoming established. They could leave the farm and now enter homes in the city. They become the pets of urbanites, the middle class, the Babbits. This is the form in which they now popped up in domestic, middle class literature—the ultimate house cat, domesticated, civilized, tranquil, wise, philosophical, and, indeed, cultivated, cultured and refined!

In his *Reineke Fox*, Goethe has the other animals recognize that tomcat Hinze alone is up to dealing with the sly old fox after the bear was badly taken in by the fox. Hinze shows his cleverness by declining the assignment, declaring that anyone else would be better than me, since I'm so little. The other animals, however, insist on it precisely because Hinze the cat is so clever and learned.

Many people would like a world of peace and friendship, like here between cat and rabbit. It's not quite as idyllic as it looks...this rabbit is simply too large and too impertinent to be this cat's prey animal.

There's a host of other German literary cats, some quite philosophical, some magical and mystical. E.T.A. Hoffman, Victor von Scheffels, Clemens von Brentano, Gottfried Keller, and Heinrich Heine are some of the other authors of those German literary cats. T.S. Eliot's *Macavity: The Mystery Cat* is an English master crook cat who always foils Scotland Yard. And the list can go on. In short, we know a great many writers of cat lore, but how about some well-known people who actually lived with cats?

FAMOUS PEOPLE & CATS

Julius Caesar was no cat lover. Nor was Nero, Hitler, Stalin, Saint Paul, Goethe, Bernard Shaw, Bach, Beethoven, Napoleon, or Eisenhower. On the other hand Emperor Hadrian was, as was Marcus Aurelius, Roosevelt, Khrushchev, Mohammed, Gottfried Keller, Heinrich Heine, Rainer Maria Rilke, Winston Churchill,Chopin, Mozart, Baudelaire, E.T.A. Hoffman, T .S. Eliot, and Ernest Hemingway. The point I'd like to make is that I preferred certain historical personages better than others even before I found out that the ones I liked were also people who liked cats. Cat haters are often power hungry and convinced of their own uniqueness (like the Caesars), whose cat-loving colleagues were considered philosopher rulers, like Marcus Aurelius,

or very human and sensitive, like Hadrian, whose love of cats inspired him to very beautiful poetry. The epigram he composed compares his soul to a cat, it is believed . It's no surprise that Hitler preferred a German Shepherd Dog to a cat.

Cat lovers are sensitive and perceptive. Cat haters are the opposite. Cat haters are very dignified and serious, while cat lovers can laugh at themselves as well as at others. Cat lovers are happy and full of vitality despite all worries. Cat haters are pessimists who are always hearing fate knocking on the door (Mozart versus Beethoven). Even a twilight personage like Cardinal Richelieu is one of us, though he didn't dance around gleefully with his enemies, but in his power politics he revealed a great deal of cat-like cleverness, self control and moderation. He had twelve kittens around all the time and cared for them lovingly. In a particularly dastardly wretched act of revenge after his death, his lifelong enemy Ludwig XIII had a few brutes of the Swiss Guard grill and eat his surviving cats.

There are numerous stories about the cats of famous people. One of the most famous is of the Prophet Mohammed and his cat Muessa. Muessa went to sleep on one of the Prophet's wide sleeves. It was the hour of prayer, which Mohammed

'Well, what about the two of us as buddies?'

had strictly enjoined the faithful to carry out. But his strictness was not so severe that he would disturb his sleeping cat just for a dogma. So he cut the sleeve of the garment off and let Muessa continue to sleep on it. Even today in Moslem countries, cats are visibly better treated than dogs.

In England and America, cats have long stood as a symbol of rationality and common sense. Sober and clean thinkers prefer cats as house companions. Isaac Newton is not only the discoverer of gravity but also the inventor of the cat door, with swinging flap, one of which graces George Washington's Mount Vernon home.

Abraham Lincoln spent an afternoon during the Civil War to find suitable quarters for three small kittens that strayed into an army camp. The British Premier Disraeli, a spirited man who had

Queen Victoria's ear, was a great cat lover. The queen, however, couldn't stand his straight-laced rival, Gladstone, a cat hater. Gladstone said spitefully that Disraeli was too much under the influence of his cat Mary, and such was not befitting a British statesman. There is no doubt that Disraeli is responsible for 19th century British post offices being issued official cats that even received salaries. Today, there are still official cats in British institutions, even at No. 10 Downing Street, official quarters for the Prime Minister.

We'll end this chapter (not because we've run out of material, but of space) with a quotation of the Italian actress Anna Magnani: 'Perhaps it would be good if cats ran the world. Then there would be enough cleverness, instinct, sensitivity, perseverance and energy at the highest official levels.'

SHOULD YOU OR NOT?

Looking back through the pages of this book frightens me a little. Have I given a balanced picture of good and bad? Did I give a true picture? Did I scare anyone from getting a cat? I hope not. In trying to be complete, I tried to include all possible problems. You can be sure, however, that many of these calamities really won't happen at all, or if they do, then not to the extent depicted in this book. I didn't write only about cat ailments and problems, but about the total cat. Part of this book is like studying accident statistics before buying a car or reading the complaint book in a restaurant instead of the usually trouble-free menu. I can assure you that most of what I and all the cat lovers I know have with our cats is immense fun and happiness.

Science has recently verified that owning and living with cats is healthy. What an argument in today's health-conscious world. I'm telling the truth. American medical investigators have clearly shown that petting and being affectionate with a cat significantly reduced blood pressure in patients with hypertension and normalized cardiac rhythm.

Another study reports on the favorable effect on depression when patients deal with cats. (Depression is *the* psychiatric condition of our time.) A woman in deep depression who sat around for twenty years without speaking a word received a kitten. In several weeks, she spoke her first words in twenty years; she told her son, 'Watch out for the kitten!'

Suggested Reading

T.F.H. Publications offers the most comprehensive selection of books dealing with cats. A selection of significant titles is presented below. They and many other works are available from your pet shop.

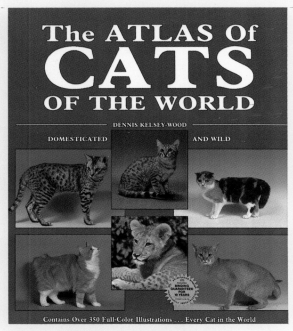

The Allure of the Cat
TS-173
304 pages
Over 400 full-color photos
10" x 14"

The Atlas of Cats of the World
TS-127
384 pages.
Over 350 full-color photos
9½ " x 12"

The Mini-Atlas of Cats
TS-152
448 pages.
Over 400 full-color photos.
5½ x 8½ "

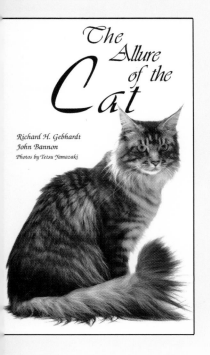

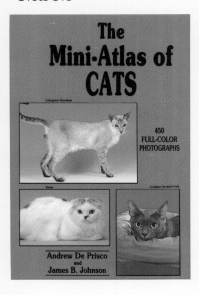

An attentive Siamese. In the cat world, the dark markings are known as *points.* They can vary somewhat in their intensity of color.

This Birman exemplifies the wide-eyed beauty of its breed.

Index